Knit your own
BOYFRIEND

Knit your own
BOYFRIEND

Create the Man You've
Been Yarning For

by Carol Meldrum

BLACK DOG
& LEVENTHAL
PUBLISHERS

Published by
Black Dog & Leventhal Publishers, Inc.
151 West 19th Street
New York, NY 10011

Distributed by
Workman Publishing Company
225 Varick Street
New York, NY 10014

Manufactured in China

Cover design by Allison Meierding

Photography by Rachel Whiting

ISBN-13: 978-1-57912-990-3

h g f e d c b a

Library of Congress Cataloging-in-Publication Data

Contents

THE PERFECT BOYFRIEND ON KNITTING

"I did this scene in a movie where I was in a room full of old ladies who were knitting, and it was an all-day scene, so they showed me how. It was one of the most relaxing days of my life. If I had to design my perfect day, that would be it. And you get something out of it at the end. You get a nice present. For someone who wants an oddly shaped, off-putting scarf."

Ryan Gosling

Basic dolls
and
hairstyles

Basic Doll

You can use this pattern to make four different doll shapes: short and slim; short and stocky; tall and slim; tall and stocky.

Height

Short doll: 10³⁄₄in (27cm)
Tall doll: 12in (30cm)

Materials

Sport-weight yarn in skin color of your choice (see right)
Pair of size 3 (3.25mm) knitting needles
Polyester toy stuffing
Tapestry and embroidery needles
Embroidery thread for eyes and mouth

Gauge

Approx 24 sts and 32 rows to 4in (10cm) over stockinette stitch using size 3 (3.25mm) needles

Skin colors

The boyfriend dolls can be made using any skin color you like. The yarn used for the skin is referred to as "yarn A" in each of the doll patterns, so it is easy to substitute a different color from the one shown if you wish. Try the following yarn shades for four different skin colors:
Rowan Cotton Glacé (100% cotton; approx 125yds/115m per 50g ball):
White skin: 725 Ecru (such as Artist, page 64)
Pale beige/pinkish skin: 730 Oyster (such as Sports Star, page 108)
Dark brown skin: 843 Toffee (such as Astronaut, page 82)
Rowan Pure Wool DK (100% super wash wool; approx 142yds/130m per 50g ball):
Light brown skin: 054 Tan (such as Surfer Dude, page 60)

These instructions are for making a naked doll. Some of the boyfriends have clothing worked as part of the basic doll by changing yarn colors. The instructions for each boyfriend specify where to change color.

Short and stocky doll   Short and slim doll

Pattern

Legs and feet

Cast on 32 sts.

Starting with a knit row, work 6 rows in stockinette stitch.

Row 7 (RS): K14, k2tog, k2togtbl, knit to end. (30 sts)

Row 8: P15, turn; slip remaining sts onto spare needle or stitch holder. Work on 15 sts only to make the left leg, working 30 rows in stockinette stitch for a short doll or 36 rows for a tall doll.

Shape left foot

Row 1 (RS): K3, m1, k1, m1, knit to end. (17 sts)

Row 2: Purl.

Row 3: K4, m1, k1, m1, knit to end. (19 sts)

Row 4: Purl.

Next row: K5, m1, k1, m1, k5, turn; do not work remaining sts on LH needle.

Next row: Slip 1, p11, turn.

Next row: Slip 1, k4, m1, k1, m1, k4, turn.

Next row: Slip 1, p9, turn.

Next row: Slip 1, k3, m1, k1, m1, k3, turn.

Next row: Slip 1, p7, turn.

Next row: Slip 1, knit to end. Bind off.

With RS facing, rejoin yarn to 15 sts on spare needle or stitch holder and work to match other leg.

Shape right foot

Row 1 (RS): K11, m1, k1, m1, knit to end. (17 sts)

Row 2: Purl.

Row 3: K12, m1, k1, m1, knit to end. (19 sts)

Row 4: Purl.

Next row: K13, m1, k1, m1, k4, turn; do not work remaining sts on the left-hand needle.

Next row: Slip 1, p10, turn.

Next row: Slip 1, k4, m1, k1, m1, k4, turn.

Next row: Slip 1, p9, turn.

Next row: Slip 1, k3, m1, k1, m1, k3, turn.

Next row: Slip 1, p8, turn.

Next row: Slip 1, knit to end. Bind off.

Short and slim doll

12

Body and head

With RS facing, pick up and knit 32 sts along cast-on edge of legs.

Row 1 (WS): Purl.

Row 2 (RS): K7, m1, k2, m1, k14, m1, k2, m1, k7. (36 sts)

Slim body shape only:

Starting and ending with a purl row, work 11 rows in stockinette stitch for a short doll or 15 rows for a tall doll.

Row 14(18): K8, m1, k2, m1, k16, m1, k2, m1, k8. (40 sts)

Starting and ending with a purl row, work 5 rows in stockinette stitch for a short doll or 7 rows for a tall doll.

Stocky body shape only:

Row 3: Purl.

Row 4: K8, m1, k2, m1, k16, m1, k2, m1, k8. (40 sts)

Row 5: Purl.

Row 6: K9, m1, k2, m1, k18, m1, k2, m1, k9. (44 sts)

Starting and ending with a purl row, work 9 rows in stockinette stitch for a short doll or 11 rows for a tall doll.

Row 16(18): K8, k2tog, k2, k2togtbl, k16, k2tog, k2, k2togtbl, k8. (40 sts)

Starting and ending with a purl row, work 3 rows in stockinette stitch for a short doll or 7 rows for a tall doll.

All dolls:

Row 20(26): K7, k2tog, k2, k2togtbl, k14, k2tog, k2, k2togtbl, k7. (36 sts)

Row 21(27): Purl.

Row 22(28): K6, k2togtbl, k2, k2tog, k12, k2togtbl, k2, k2tog, k6. (32 sts)

Row 23(29): Purl.

Row 24(30): K5, k2tog, k2, k2togtbl, k10, k2tog, k2, k2togtbl, k5. (28 sts)

Row 25(31): P4, p2togtbl, p2, p2tog, p8, p2togtbl, p2, p2tog, p4. (24 sts)

Row 26(32): K3, k2tog, k2, k3togtbl, k4, k3tog, k2, k2togtbl, k3. (18 sts)

Neck and head

Starting and ending with a purl row, work 3 rows in stockinette stitch.

Start shaping head as follows:

Row 1 (RS): K4, m1, k2, m1, k6, m1, k2, m1, k4. (22 sts)

Row 2: P5, m1, p2, m1, p8, m1, p2, m1, p5. (26 sts)

Row 3: K6, m1, k2, m1, k10, m1, k2, m1, k6. (30 sts)

Starting and ending with a purl row, work 11 rows in stockinette stitch.

Row 15: K5, k2tog, k2, k2togtbl, k8, k2tog, k2, k2togtbl, k5. (26 sts)

Row 16: P4, p2togtbl, p2, p2tog, p6, p2togtbl, p2, p2tog, p4. (22 sts)

Row 17: K3, k2tog, k2, k2togtbl, k4, k2tog, k2, k2togtbl, k3. (18 sts)

Break off yarn and thread through stitches on needle, but do not pull tight.

Arm and hand (make 2)

Cast on 12 sts.

Starting with a knit row, work 26 rows in stockinette stitch for a short doll or 30 rows for a tall doll.

Shape hand

Next row (RS): K1, [k2tog] twice, k2, [k2tog] twice, k1. (8 sts)

Next row: Purl.
Next row: K2, [m1, k2] to end. (11 sts)
Next row: Purl.
Next row: K2, m1, k3, m1, k4, m1, k2. (14 sts)
Starting and ending with a purl row, work 5 rows in stockinette stitch.
Next row: K1, [k2tog] to last st, k1. (8 sts)
Break off yarn and thread through stitches on needle. Pull tight and secure the end.

Sole of foot (make 2)

Cast on 3 sts.
Row 1: Knit.
Row 2: K1, m1, k1, m1, k1. (5 sts)
Knit 13 rows.
Row 16: K2tog, k1, k2tog. (3 sts)
Row 17: Knit.
Bind off.

Finishing

Use the pictures as a guide throughout the finishing of all pieces. Sew seams using mattress stitch (page 128) or whip stitch (page 129), and use matching yarn unless stated otherwise. Weave in all loose ends, using seams where appropriate, and block and press pieces if required. When inserting stuffing, use a chopstick or similar tool to help push it right down into the hands and feet. You can sculpt the doll's body shape by varying the quantity of stuffing and how you position it, but take care not to overstuff.

Legs and feet

Sew side edges of each leg and foot together to form inner leg seams. Sew back seam on doll's bottom, then sew soles to base of feet. Insert stuffing into legs and feet.

Body and head

Sew back seam on body, then insert stuffing down through head. Sew back seam on head, then insert stuffing. Pull thread at top of head tight and secure with a few stitches.

To define neck, thread tapestry needle with length of yarn but do not secure or tie knot. Insert needle at back seam just under first row of increasing for head. Weave in and out of stitches around neck. Pull tight and tie a double knot, then sew in loose ends.

Arms

Sew side edges of each arm together to form underarm seams. Insert stuffing, then sew up the top opening. Sew arms to body, using shaping marks on shoulders to position them symmetrically.

Hair and face

Hair: Choose a hairstyle (page 18), then follow the instructions to make it and sew it onto the doll's head.
Eyes: Work French knots (page 129), using embroidery thread wrapped around needle 5 times (any color you like).
Mouth: Work in backstitch (page 129) using red embroidery thread.
Facial hair: Add facial hair if desired (page 27).

Hair's Your Type

Which coif for your guy?

Sporty Guys

Super hot or jock
Sports star
- Slicked back/Short back and sides (for wash 'n' go)
- Bald (no wash, just go)
- Curly (watch it grow)
- Messy and tousled (get up and go)

So cool, it's hot
Surfer dude/Skateboarder
- Slicked back (gelled like it's already wet)
- Peaked cut/Shoulder length/Dreadlocks (great on selfies)
- Soft crop (let it go with the flow)

Stubble? No trouble
Giving your man hipster or sports guy fuzz is as easy as 1, 2, 3 (turns around the needle). See page 27.

Career Guys

Dorky
Nerd
- Short back and sides/Side parting (IT office guys are not "it")
- Curly/Shoulder length/Ponytail/Dreadlocks (anything goes for the home alone hacker/gamer in his PJs)

Mainstream
Businessman
- Slicked back (for the Wall Street wolf)
- Short back and sides (vintage Mad Men for those intimidating boardroom moments)

Caring
Doctor
- Side parting/Short back and sides/whatever (who cares about hair when you can get lost in those Dr McDreamy baby blues)

Macho Men

Legend
Fireman
- Short back and sides/Side parting (so he doesn't get "hat hair")
- Bald/Short Afro (ditto)

Superhero
- Slicked back (for full flying-through-the-air effect)
- Short back and sides (for vintage superhero and now current trend look)
- Neat 1950s quiff (retro is so now)

Brave and a bit mad
Astronaut
- Slicked back/Side parting (practical under helmet)
- Short Afro/Bald (ditto) with mustache (at least it can be seen through the visor)
- Never long, as zero gravity takes "hair-raising" to a new level

Outdoorsman
- Shoulder length (there are no clippers or gel in the jungle)
- Dreadlocks/Cornrows (he's ditched the brush and hair products to keep backpack weight down)
- Mustache ("Dr Livingstone, I presume" for the Victorian explorer look)
- Stubble (for striking matches against to light the campfire)

Cool Dudes

Urban
Hip-hop guy
- Cornrows/Dreadlocks (for shaking and swinging when he's rapping and DJing)
- Slicked back (perfect under back-to-front baseball cap)

Artsy
Artist
- Ponytail ('cos he's like, really radical and non-conformist)
- Goatee (when the hairs on his brush fall out he can always pluck a few from his beard)

Rock star
- Soft crop (for the boyband look)
- Messed-up 1950s quiff (chanelling Elvis and a hundred others)
- Dreadlocks (Bob Marley rules)
- Shoulder length (add sideburns for the full-on 70s rock star)
- Stubble (night is day, day is night, who has time to, like, shave?)

Indie
Hipster
- Short back and sides, long on top (über-cool)
- Beard (nouveau full beard for the natural, manly look)
- Strategically tousled (the intellectu-wool look)

Hairstyles

Here are 15 hairstyles to choose from, plus some ideas for facial hair.

Materials

Yarn in color of your choice; sport-weight yarn is used unless stated otherwise, but you can vary the yarn weight to achieve finer or thicker hair as desired
Pair of size 3 (3.25mm) knitting needles
Tapestry needle
Crochet hook for some hairstyles (see instructions)
Embroidery needle and thread for stubble

Bald

Take the easy option and make yourself a bald boyfriend. Probably best not to add a comb over...

Short hairstyles

Short back and sides

Cast on 9 sts.
Row 1 (WS): Purl.
Row 2 (RS): K1, m1, knit to last st, m1, k1. (11 sts)
Row 3: P1, m1, purl to last st, m1, p1. (13 sts)
Row 4: Knit.
Row 5: Purl.
Row 6: As row 2. (15 sts)
Row 7: As row 3. (17 sts)
Row 8: Cast on 2 sts, knit to end. (19 sts)
Row 9: Cast on 2 sts, purl to end. (21 sts)
Row 10: Knit.
Row 11: Purl.
Row 12: K2, [k2togtbl, k3] 3 times, k2togtbl, k2. (17 sts)
Row 13: Purl.
Row 14: K1, [k2togtbl, k2] to end. (13 sts)
Row 15: Purl.
Row 16: K1, [k2togtbl, k1] to end. (9 sts)
Knit 4 rows.
Bind off.
Pin and stitch hair to doll's head, with bound-off edge toward top of head.

Afro

Using worsted-weight yarn, cast on 4 sts. Knit 10 rows.

Row 11: K1, m1, k2, m1, k1. (6 sts)

Continue knitting every row until strip fits from top of head to back of neck. Bind off.

Pin and stitch hair to doll's head, with bound-off edge toward top of head.

Work a few French knots around hairline (yarn wrapped around needle 3 times).

Side parting

Cast on 9 sts and work rows 1–7 as for short back and sides hairstyle.

Row 8 (RS): Cast on 3 sts, knit to end. (20 sts)

Row 9: Cast on 4 sts, purl to end. (24 sts)

Row 10: Knit.

Row 11: As row 9. (28 sts)

Row 12: K1, [k2togtbl, k2] 6 times, k2togtbl, k1. (21 sts)

Row 13: Purl.

Row 14: K1, [k2togtbl, k1] twice, k2togtbl, k3, [k2tog, k1] 3 times. (15 sts)

Row 15: P1, [p2tog] 3 times, p1, [p2togtbl] 3 times, p1. (9 sts)

Break off yarn and thread through stitches on needle. Pull tight and secure the end.

Pin and stitch hair to doll's head, with bound-off edge toward top of head.

Slicked back

Curly

Side parting

1950s quiff

Cast on 13 sts.

Starting with a knit row, work 4 rows in stockinette stitch.

Row 5 (RS): K1, m1, knit to last st, m1, k1. (15 sts)

Row 6: Purl.

Repeat last 2 rows five times more. (25 sts)

Row 17: K1, m1, knit to end. (26 sts)

Row 18: Purl.

Repeat last 2 rows once more. (27 sts)

Row 21: [K4, k2tog] twice, k3, [k2tog, k4] twice. (23 sts)

Row 22: Purl.

Row 23: K3, [k2tog, k3] to end. (19 sts)

Row 24: Purl.

Row 25: K3, [k2tog, k2] to end. (15 sts)

Row 26: Purl.

Row 27: K2, [k2tog, k1] to last st, k1. (11 sts)

Break off yarn and thread through stitches on needle. Pull tight and secure the end.

Pin and stitch hair to doll's head, with bound-off edge toward top of head. Wrap a length of yarn around a couple of fingers, then place it on top front of head and stitch into place to produce a neat quiff or messed-up bed-head look.

Peaked cut
Hair base

Using fingering-weight yarn, cast on 11 sts. Starting with a knit row, work 4 rows in stockinette stitch.

Bald with stubble

Neat 1950s quiff

Shoulder length, mustache, and sideburns

Row 5 (RS): K1, m1, knit to last st, m1, k1. (13 sts)

Row 6: Purl.

Repeat last 2 rows once more. (15 sts)

Starting with a knit row, work 2 rows in stockinette stitch.

Repeat rows 5–6 twice more. (19 sts)

Row 15: K2, k2togtbl, knit to last 2 sts, k2tog. (17 sts)

Row 16: Purl.

Repeat last 2 rows twice more, then row 15 once again. (11 sts)

Row 22: P2, p2tog, purl to last 3 sts, p2togtbl, p1. (9 sts)

Row 23: As row 15. (7 sts)

Bind off knitwise, working k2togtbl at beginning of bind-off and k2tog at end. Pin and stitch hair base to doll's head, with bound-off edge toward top of head.

Peaked top

Cut 5in (12.5cm) lengths of sport-weight yarn and divide into eight sections of 3 strands.

Insert a crochet hook under a stitch at center front of hair base just behind bound-off edge, fold a section of hair in half and pull it through to form a loop, then pass the cut ends of the strands through the loop and pull tight to form a tassel. Repeat to add another tassel on each side of first tassel on bound-off edge. Add two more tassels just behind and to either side of the first tassel. Add two more tassels behind these, one slightly to the right and one slightly to the left, then add a final tassel in between the last two. Trim hair into required shape.

Long hairstyles

Shoulder length

Hair base

Cast on 9 sts.

Row 1 (WS): Purl.

Row 2 (RS): K1, m1, knit to last st, m1, k1. (11 sts)

Row 3: Purl.

Repeat last 2 rows three times more. (17 sts)

Row 10: Knit.

Row 11: Purl.

Row 12: As row 2. (19 sts)

Row 13: P1, m1, purl to last st, m1, p1. (21 sts)

Row 14: K2, [k2togtbl, k3] 3 times, k2togtbl, k2. (17 sts)

Row 15: Purl.

Row 16: K1, [k2togtbl, k2] to end. (13 sts)

Row 17: Purl.

Row 18: K1, [k2togtbl, k1] to end. (9 sts)

Row 19: P1, p2tog, p3, p2togtbl, p1. (7 sts)

Row 20: K1, k2togtbl, k1, k2tog, k1. (5 sts)

Bind off.

Pin and stitch hair base to doll's head, with bound-off edge toward top of head.

Long strands

Cut thirty 6in (15cm) lengths of yarn. Lay the strands across the hair base and pin in place. Using matching yarn, work backstitch from top of head to neckline to secure strands and create center parting.

Ponytail

Using worsted-weight yarn, make a hair base as for shoulder-length hairstyle and stitch to doll's head.

For the ponytail, cut 12in (30cm) lengths of worsted-weight yarn and divide into nine sections of 2-3 strands. Attach the strands along top front seam of hair base by inserting a crochet hook under a stitch, folding a section of hair in half and pulling it through to form a loop, then pass the cut ends of the strands through the loop and pull tight to form a tassel.

Gather into a bunch at back of head and use a length of yarn to tie into a ponytail. Trim the ponytail if you want it shorter.

Slicked back

Make a hair base as for shoulder-length hairstyle and stitch to doll's head. Cut 3¼in (8cm) lengths of yarn and divide into nine sections of 2 strands. Attach the strands to the hair base as for a ponytail. Slick the strands back over the hair base and work a few stitches at back of head to secure.

Dreadlocks

Using fingering-weight yarn, make a hair base as for shoulder-length hairstyle and stitch to doll's head.

Using super bulky yarn, cut nine 5½in (14cm) lengths for bottom layer of dreadlocks and twelve 7in (18cm) lengths for top layer. Fold each strand in half. Thread tapestry needle with fingering-weight yarn. Inserting needle through fold of yarn, thread all of the shorter dreadlocks onto the needle. Slide the strands together so that the layer is 3½in (9cm) wide. Pin the layer around head, approx 1½in (4cm) from center

Dreadlocks

Short back and sides

top, and stitch into position. Thread all of the longer dreadlocks together as before, slide together so that the top layer is 4in (10cm) wide and then tie the fingering-weight yarn to form a loop. Fold the loop in half, pin along top of head in a slightly off-center diagonal and stitch into position.

Curly
Special abbreviation: L1 = loop 1: insert RH needle into stitch as if to knit, wrap yarn over and around RH needle point and forefinger twice, then over and around RH needle point once more; draw all 3 loops through st and slip onto LH needle, then insert RH needle through back of these 3 loops and original st and ktogtbl.
Cast on 9 sts.
Row 1 (RS): Knit.
Row 2: K1, m1, knit to last st, m1, k1. (11 sts)

Row 3: As row 2. (13 sts)
Knit 2 rows.
Row 6: As row 2. (15 sts)
Row 7: L1, m1, [L1, k1] 6 times, L1, m1, L1. (17 sts)
Row 8: Cast on 2 sts, knit to end. (19 sts)
Row 9: Cast on 2 sts, [k1, L1] to last st, k1. (21 sts)
Row 10: Knit.
Row 11: L1, [k1, L1] to end.
Row 12: K2, [k2togtbl, k3] 3 times, k2togtbl, k2. (17 sts)
Row 13: K1, [L1, k1] to end.
Row 14: K1, [k2togtbl, k2] to end. (13 sts)
Row 15: As row 11.
Row 16: K1, [k2togtbl, k1] to end. (9 sts)
Row 17: As row 13.
Row 18: Knit.
Bind off.
Pin and stitch hair to doll's head, with bound-off edge toward top of head.

Ponytail with goatee

Afro

Messed-up 1950s quiff

Cornrows

Using a crochet hook, make five lengths of 25 chain stitches and four lengths of 22 chain stitches.

Starting with the longer chains, pin first chain down center of head, from top of brow toward back of neck. Sew in place, leaving the long end of the chain loose from the neck downward. Pin and sew another two long chains on each side of the first one. Repeat to stitch two shorter chains on each side of the head.

Messy and tousled

Hair base

Cast on 13 sts.

Row 1 (RS): Knit.

Row 2: Purl.

Row 3: K1, m1, knit to last st, m1, k1. (15 sts)

Row 4: Purl.

Repeat last 2 rows once more. (17 sts)

Row 7: As row 3. (19 sts)

Row 8: P1, m1, purl to last st, m1, p1. (21 sts)

Repeat last 2 rows once more. (25 sts)

Cast on 14 sts, then knit to end. (39 sts)

Starting and ending with a purl row, work 3 rows in stockinette stitch.

Row 15: K5, k2tog, [k4, k2tog] to last 2 sts, k2. (33 sts)

Row 16: Purl.

Row 17: K4, k2tog, [k3, k2tog] to last 2 sts, k2. (27 sts)

Row 18: P2, [p2tog, p2] to last 5 sts, p2tog, p3. (21 sts)

Row 19: K2, [k2tog, k1] to last 4 sts, k2tog, k2. (15 sts)

Row 20: [P2tog] to last st, p1. (9 sts)

Break off yarn and thread through stitches on needle. Pull tight and secure the end.

Sew the open side edges together.

Pin and stitch hair base to doll's head, with cast-on edge toward back of neck.

Long strands

Cut 4in (10cm) lengths of yarn and divide into seven sections of 2 strands. Insert a crochet hook under a stitch at center top of hair base, fold a section of hair in half and pull it through to form a loop, then pass the cut ends of the strands through the loop and pull tight to form a tassel. Repeat to add tassels evenly around crown of head.

Trim hair into required style, unravel some of the strands to create a slightly curly look and secure with a few stitches if required.

Hipster hair

Hair base

Cast on 13 sts and work rows 1–10 as for messy and tousled hairstyle. (25 sts)

Cast on 12 sts, then knit to end. (37 sts)

Starting and ending with a purl row, work 3 rows in stockinette stitch.

Row 15: [K4, k2tog] to last st, k1. (31 sts)

Row 16: Purl.

Row 17: [K3, k2tog] to last st, k1. (25 sts)

Row 18: P1, [p2tog, p2] to end. (19 sts)

Row 19: [K1, k2tog] to last st, k1. (13 sts)

Row 20: P1, [p2tog] to end. (7 sts)

Break off yarn and thread through

stitches on needle. Pull tight and secure the end.

Pin and stitch hair base to doll's head, with initial cast-on edge toward back of neck and the open side edges of hair base forming a side parting.

Long strands

Cut 6in (15cm) lengths of yarn and divide into fourteen sections of 3 strands.

Insert a crochet hook under a stitch at top of hair parting on hair base, fold a section of hair in half and pull it through to form a loop, then pass the cut ends of the strands through the loop and pull tight to form a tassel. Repeat twice more along hair parting, down toward front of head. Add three more rows of tassels along top of head, offsetting each row, and sweep them all to one side over top of head. Add final two tassels along other side of hair parting. Unravel some of the strands to give the hair a slightly curly look, then stitch into desired style.

Soft crop
Hair base

Using fingering-weight yarn, cast on 13 sts. Starting with a knit row, work 4 rows in stockinette stitch.

Row 5 (RS): K1, m1, knit to last st, m1, k1. (15 sts)

Row 6: Purl.

Repeat last 2 rows three times more. (21 sts)

Cast on 10 sts, then knit to end. (31 sts)

Row 14: Purl.

Row 15: [K4, k2tog] to last st, k1. (26 sts)

Row 16: Purl.

Row 17: [K3, k2tog] to last st, k1. (21 sts)

Row 18: P1, [p2tog, p2] to end. (16 sts)

Cornrows

Soft crop

Hipster hair and beard

Row 19: [K1, k2tog] to last st, k1. (11 sts)
Break off yarn and thread through stitches on needle. Pull tight and secure the end.

Pin and stitch hair base to doll's head, with initial cast-on edge toward back of neck and the open side edges of hair base forming a side parting.

Long strands

Cut 5in (12.5cm) lengths of fingering-weight yarn and divide into eleven sections of 3 strands.

Insert a crochet hook under a stitch at top of hair parting on hair base, fold a section of hair in half and pull it through to form a loop, then pass the cut ends of the strands through the loop and pull tight to form a tassel. Repeat twice more along hair parting, down toward front of head. Add two more rows of tassels along top of head, offsetting each row. Add final two tassels along other side of hair parting and sweep over to other side of head. Trim hair into required style and secure with a few stitches if required.

TIPS FOR BOYFRIENDS DISPLAYING EARLY SIGNS OF MALE-PATTERN BALDNESS

1. Comb over (nah, not unless he's 40+)

2. Buzz cut (so short the bald bit is less noticeable)

3. A complete shave (be bald, bold, and ballsy/proud, it didn't do LL Cool J and Bruce Willis any harm)

4. A weave (if he's sports star/movie star rich)

5. A wig shop (last stitch attempt)

Facial hair

Goatee

Cast on 5 sts.
Row 1: Purl.
Row 2: K1, k3tog, k1. (3 sts)
Row 3: Purl.
Row 4: K3tog.
Fasten off.
Pin and stitch onto doll's face just under mouth.

Stubble

Using embroidery thread, work French knots around mouth and jaw (wrapped around needle 3 times).

Mustache

Cast on 11 sts.
Row 1: K1, slip 1, k2tog, psso, k3, k3tog, k1. (7 sts)
Bind off 1 st, k3tog, pass bound-off st over k3tog just worked, bind off remaining stitches.
Pin and stitch onto doll's face just above mouth.

Beard

Cast on 20 sts.
Row 1: Knit.
Row 2: K8, bind off 4 sts, knit to end. (Two sections of 8 sts)
Row 3: Bind off 2 sts, knit until there are 8 sts on right-hand needle, turn, cast on 5 sts using two-needle method, turn, knit to end. (19 sts)
Row 4: Bind off 2 sts, knit to end. (17 sts)
Row 5: K1, [k2tog] twice, k7, [k2tog] twice, k1. (13 sts)
Row 6: K11, turn.
Row 7: Slip 1, k8, turn.
Row 8: Slip 1, k5, turn.
Row 9: Slip 1, k3, turn.
Row 10: Slip 1, k2, turn.
Row 11: Knit.
Bind off.
The cast-on edge is the top (mustache). Pin center top of beard to just above mouth, making sure that the beard opening aligns with the embroidered mouth. Sew beard in place, leaving bottom of beard unsewn over chin.

Sideburns (make 2)

Cast on 5 sts.
Row 1: Bind off 2 sts, knit to end.
Bind off remaining sts.
Pin and stitch onto doll's face, making sure that they are positioned symmetrically.

Clothing

T-shirt and Jeans

The classic combo that most boys never grow out of wearing. If you prefer your boyfriend in baggy jeans, see page 90.

Materials

Old T-shirt or 8in (20cm) square of jersey fabric
Old jeans or 10in (25cm) square of denim fabric (or use another fabric for a different look)
Sharp sewing needle
Thread to match T-shirt fabric, plus white and orange for jeans

Instructions

Jeans

Using template on page 131, cut out front and back of trousers from denim fabric. If you want your jeans to have a turn-up, add an extra ³⁄₈–⁵⁄₈in (1-1.5cm) at the bottom. Using ¹⁄₄in (5mm) seam allowance and backstitch, pin the pieces RS together and sew side seams and then inner leg seams. Turn RS out.

Waistband

Cut a 1¹⁄₄in (3cm) wide strip of denim long enough to go around top of trousers with a ³⁄₈in (1cm) overlap at front. Fold the fabric lengthways into three sections, like an envelope. Using orange thread, sew a line of running stitch slightly in from top and bottom folds.

If using old jeans, cut the waistband from the bottom hem to utilize the contrast stitching.

Pin waistband around top of trousers, starting at center front and allowing the other end to overlap. If using an old jeans hem as the waistband, pin so that raw edge of denim shows on RS. Sew waistband in place using hem stitch or backstitch.

Fly

Cut a ³/₈ x 1¹/₂in (1 x 4cm) strip of denim for the fly. If using old jeans, use a 1¹/₂in (4cm) long section from belt loops. Pin to front of trousers, directly below waistband overlap, and stitch into position.

T-shirt

Front and back (alike)

If using an old T-shirt, cut two 4in (10cm) squares using the existing hem for your hem. Otherwise, cut two rectangles 4in (10cm) wide and 5¹/₂in (14cm) deep. With WS facing, fold up ³/₄in (2cm) at bottom edge of each square, then fold up again. Pin and stitch into position.

Long sleeves

If using an old T-shirt, cut two rectangles 4in (10cm) wide and 3¹/₂in (9cm) deep using the existing hem for your hem. If not, cut two rectangles 4in (10cm) wide and 4¹/₄in (11cm) deep. Fold up ³/₈in (1cm) at bottom edge of each rectangle, then fold up again. Pin and stitch into position.

Short sleeves

Cut two rectangles 4in (10cm) wide and 2in (5cm) deep. Fold the sleeves in half lengthways and press with steam iron.

Finishing

Using ¹/₄in (5mm) seam allowance and backstitch, pin front and back pieces RS together and then sew shoulder seams by sewing along each side of top edge for approx ³/₄in (2cm), leaving the center unsewn for the neck opening. Open out so that front and back are lying flat, then pin sleeves in place, aligning center of sleeves with shoulder seams. Sew sleeves to body. Sew up the side and sleeve seams.

Alternative

For a shaped neck and three-quarter-length sleeves, see page 72.

Shorts

Show off your boyfriend's legs in a pair of casual or smart shorts, or hide them by lengthening the shorts to adapt them into trousers.

Materials

Beach shorts

Two 5¹/₂in (14cm) squares of brightly colored cotton fabric
Sharp sewing needle and matching thread
8in (20cm) cord elastic

Tailored shorts

Old pair of khaki green army trousers or 16in (40cm) square of utility-weight polycotton khaki fabric
Sharp sewing needle and matching thread
Press stud

Instructions

Beach shorts

With WS facing, fold up ⁵/₈in (1.5cm) at bottom edge of first square of fabric, then fold up again and press with steam iron. Sew along fold using hem stitch. Repeat with other square of fabric.
Measuring from top edge, mark a point 3in (7.5cm) down both side edges of each piece of fabric. With RS together and using ³/₈in (1cm) seam allowance and backstitch, sew fabric together from top edge to 3in (7.5cm) marks.

Waistband

To form channel for elastic at waist, fold down ⁵/₈in (1.5cm) from top edge, then fold down again and press with steam iron. Sew around channel, just above the folded edge, leaving a small gap for elastic to be threaded through.
With RS together, align seams at center front and back, then sew from center seam to bottom hem on both inside legs.

Finishing

Attach safety pin to end of elastic. Insert

pin into the gap in waistband channel and thread through. Bring ends of elastic together, place shorts on doll and pull elastic tight so that shorts fit snugly around waist. Knot the ends together and trim off excess elastic.

Tailored shorts

Using template on page 132, cut two pieces of fabric for legs of shorts. If using an old pair of trousers, use existing hem and cut fabric to second fold line on template.

If using fabric, hem as follows:

With WS facing, fold up ¾in (2cm) at bottom edge of first leg, then fold up again and press with steam iron. Sew along fold using hem stitch. Repeat with other leg.

Joining fabric

Measuring from top edge, mark a point 2in (5cm) down both side edges of each leg. With RS together and using ¼in (5mm) seam allowance and backstitch, sew fabric together from top edge to 2in (5cm) marks.

With RS together, align seams at center front and back, then sew from center seam to bottom hem on both legs. Place shorts on doll, then fold a ⅜in (1cm) pleat at front of waist on each leg; the pleats should be symmetrical and fold out toward the sides. Pin and stitch down edge of each pleat for 1¼in (3cm).

Waistband

Cut a 1½in (4cm) wide strip of fabric long enough to go around top of shorts with a ⅜in (1cm) overlap at front. Fold the fabric lengthways into three sections, like an envelope. Using point of a knitting needle or similar tool, tuck in open ends of fabric strip and sew together.

Pin waistband around top of shorts, starting at center front and allowing the other end to overlap. Sew waistband in place using hem stitch or backstitch. Sew one half of press stud to inside of overlap. Place shorts on doll, position other half of press stud on waistband to achieve a snug fit, and sew in place.

Raglan Sweater

Keep your boyfriend warm and cosy in a snuggly knitted sweater.

Raglan sweater

Materials

Rowan Felted Tweed DK (50% merino wool, 25% alpaca, 25% viscose; approx 191yds/175m per 50g ball):
  1 ball in 173 Duck Egg (A)
  1 ball in 150 Rage (B)
Pair of size 3 (3.25mm) knitting needles
Tapestry needle

Gauge

Approx 24 sts and 32 rows to 4in (10cm) over stockinette stitch using size 3 (3.25mm) needles

Fair Isle sweater

Follow the charts on page 132 to make a Fair Isle raglan sweater, working in stockinette stitch unless indicated otherwise. Change colors as shown.

Pattern

Front and back (alike)

Using B, cast on 21 sts.
Break off B and join in A.
Row 1 (RS): K1, [p1, k1] to end.
Row 2: P1, [k1, p1] to end.
Starting with a knit row, work 20 rows in stockinette stitch.
Place marker at beginning and end of row.
Row 23: K2, k2togtbl, knit to last 4 sts, k2tog, k2. (19 sts)
Row 24: Purl.
Repeat last 2 rows four times more. (11 sts)
Do not bind off; slip stitches onto spare needle or stitch holder.

Sleeves (make 2)

Using B, cast on 15 sts.
Break off B and join in A.
Row 1 (RS): K1, [p1, k1] to end.
Row 2: P1, [k1, p1] to end.
Starting with a knit row, work 20 rows in stockinette stitch.
Place marker at beginning and end of row.
Row 23: K2, k2togtbl, knit to last 4 sts, k2tog, k2. (13 sts)
Row 24: Purl.
Repeat last 2 rows twice more. (9 sts)
Row 29: K2, k2togtbl, k1, k2tog, k2. (7 sts)
Row 30: Purl.
Row 31: K2, slip 2, k1, p2sso, k2. (5 sts)
Row 32: Purl.
Do not bind off; slip stitches onto spare needle or stitch holder.

Neckband

With RS facing, slip pieces onto left-hand needle in following sequence: front, sleeve, back, sleeve. (32 sts)
Join in A.
Row 1 (RS): [P1, k1] twice, p2tog, [k1, p1] 4 times, k1, p2tog, k1, p1, k1, p2tog, [k1, p1] 5 times. (29 sts)
Row 2: K1, [p1, k1] to end.
Break off A and join in B.
Row 3: P1, [k1, p1] to end.
Bind off.

Finishing

Weave in loose ends. Block and press if required. Using mattress stitch, sew up the raglan seams of body and sleeves between markers. Sew up side seams and sleeves.

WHY A KNITTED
BOYFRIEND IS BETTER
THAN A REAL BOYFRIEND

1. He never says no to a cuddle.
2. He never answers you back.
3. He's good at washing up (he's ultra absorbent).

Jumper and Hoodie

Hug your hoodie boyfriend all you want in these smart knits.

Materials

Rowan Cotton Glacé (100% cotton; approx 125yds/115m per 50g ball):
  1 ball in 831 Dawn Grey (A)
  1 ball in 829 Twilight (B) for stripey jumper only
Pair of size 3 (3.25mm) knitting needles
Tapestry needle
Small button, sharp sewing needle, and gray thread for stripey jumper

Gauge

Approx 24 sts and 32 rows to 4in (10cm) over stockinette stitch using size 3 (3.25mm) needles

Patterns

Stripey jumper
Front and back (alike)
Using A, cast on 22 sts.
Row 1 (RS): K2, [p2, k2] to end.
Row 2: P2, [k2, p2] to end.
Starting with a knit row, work 24 rows in stockinette stitch, changing colors for stripes as follows: 6 rows in A, [2 rows in B, 2 rows in A] 4 times, 2 rows in A.
Place marker at beginning and end of row.
Continue using A only as follows:
Row 27: K2, k2tog, knit to last 4 sts, k2togtbl, k2. (20 sts)
Row 28: Purl.
Repeat last 2 rows five times more. (10 sts)
Do not bind off; slip remaining sts onto spare needle or stitch holder.

Sleeves (make 2)
Using A, cast on 18 sts.
Row 1 (RS): K2, [p2, k2] to end.
Row 2: P2, [k2, p2] to end.
Starting with a knit row, work 22 rows in stockinette stitch, changing colors for stripes as follows: 6 rows in A, [2 rows in B, 2 rows in A] 4 times.
Place marker at beginning and end of row.
Continue using A only as follows:
Row 25: K2, k2tog, knit to last 4 sts, k2togtbl, k2. (16 sts)
Row 26: Purl.
Repeat last 2 rows five times more. (6 sts)
Do not bind off; slip remaining sts onto spare needle or stitch holder.

Neckband

With RS facing, slip pieces onto left-hand needle in following sequence: front, sleeve, back, sleeve. (32 sts)

Row 1 (RS): Knit.
Row 2: Purl.
Row 3: Knit.
Bind off knitwise.

Finishing

Weave in loose ends. Block and press if required. Using mattress stitch, sew up three of the armhole seams of body and sleeves between markers, leaving the front right armhole seam open. Sew up side seams and sleeves.

Attach a small loop of yarn to the top of the open armhole seam on one side, then sew a button to the opposite side to correspond with the button loop.

Hoodie

Back

Using A, cast on 22 sts.

Row 1 (RS): K2, [p2, k2] to end.
Row 2: P2, [k2, p2] to end.
Starting with a knit row, work 24 rows in stockinette stitch.
Place marker at beginning and end of row.
Row 27: K2, k2tog, knit to last 4 sts, k2togtbl, k2. (20 sts)
Row 28: Purl.
Repeat last 2 rows five times more. (10 sts)
Do not bind off; slip remaining sts onto spare needle or stitch holder.

Right front

Using A, cast on 12 sts.

Row 1 (RS): K4, [p2, k2] to end.

Row 2: [P2, k2] to end.

Row 3: Knit.

Row 4: Purl to last 2 sts, k2.

Repeat last 2 rows eleven times more.

Place marker at beginning and end of row.

Row 27: Knit to last 4 sts, k2tog, k2. (10 sts)

Row 28: As row 4.

Repeat last 2 rows twice more. (6 sts)

Do not bind off; slip remaining sts onto spare needle or stitch holder.

Left front

Using A, cast on 12 sts.

Row 1 (RS): K2, [p2, k2] to last 2 sts, k2.

Row 2: [K2, p2] to end.

Row 3: Knit.

Row 4: K2, purl to end.

Repeat last 2 rows eleven times more.

Place marker at beginning and end of row.

Row 27: K2, k2togtbl, knit to end. (10 sts)

Row 28: As row 4.

Repeat last 2 rows twice more. (6 sts)

Do not bind off; slip remaining sts onto spare needle or stitch holder.

Sleeves (make 2)

Using A, cast on 18 sts.

Row 1 (RS): K2, [p2, k2] to end.

Row 2: P2, [k2, p2] to end.

Starting with a knit row, work 22 rows in stockinette stitch.

Place marker at beginning and end of row.

Row 25: K2, k2tog, knit to last 4 sts, k2togtbl, k2. (16 sts)

Row 26: Purl.

Repeat last 2 rows five times more. (6 sts)

Do not bind off; slip remaining sts onto spare needle or stitch holder.

Neckline and hood

With RS facing, slip pieces onto left-hand needle in following sequence: left front, sleeve, back, sleeve, right front. (34 sts)

Row 1 (RS): K4, k2togtbl, k2tog, k2, k2togtbl, k2tog, k6, k2togtbl, k2tog, k2, k2togtbl, k2tog, k4. (26 sts)

Row 2: K2, purl to last 2 sts, k2.

Row 3: Knit.

Repeat rows 2–3 five times more, then row 2 once again.

Row 15: K11, k2togtbl, k2tog, knit to end. (24 sts)

Row 16: K2, purl to last 2 sts, k2.

Row 17: K10, k2togtbl, k2tog, knit to end. (22 sts)

Row 18: K2, p7, p2tog, p2togtbl, p7, k2. (20 sts)

Row 19: K10, leaving remaining 10 sts on left-hand needle.

Fold work in half with RS together and bind off using three-needle method.

Finishing

Weave in loose ends. Block and press if required. Using mattress stitch, sew up the armhole seams of body and sleeves between markers. Sew up side seams and sleeves.

Smart Jacket

A smart but casual choice that is perfectly on-trend. For a matching waistcoat, see page 116.

Materials

9 x 12in (23 x 30cm) sheet of felt fabric
Press stud
Small button
Sharp sewing needle and thread
to match felt and button colors

Instructions

Using templates on pages 140-141, cut out back, left front, right front, two sleeves, and two pocket tops from felt fabric. With RS together and using $^1/_4$in (5mm) seam allowance and backstitch, pin and sew front and back pieces together along sloped shoulder seams.

Turn RS out, fold back the lapels and gently press with steam iron. Open out the front and back sections with WS facing. Pin top sloped edges of sleeves into position, aligning center top of sleeves with shoulder seams, and sew together. Pin and sew side seams and sleeve seams, then turn RS out and press with steam iron.

Sew press stud just below lapels so that left front overlaps right front of jacket. Sew button onto left front on outside of jacket. Sew pocket tops into position.

Knitted Jacket

Make your boyfriend look hot and cool at the same time with these funky knitted jackets. For a knitted business suit jacket, see page 94.

Materials

Green jacket (main pattern):
Rowan Tweed (100% wool; approx 129yds/118m per 50g ball):
   1 ball in 589 Hubberholme
Gray jacket (variation):
Rowan Felted Tweed DK (50% merino wool, 25% alpaca, 25% viscose; approx 191yds/175m per 50g ball):
   1 ball in 172 Ancient
Pair of size 3 (3.25mm) knitting needles
Tapestry needle

Gauge

Approx 24 sts and 32 rows to 4in (10cm) over stockinette stitch using size 3 (3.25mm) needles

Pattern

Back and sleeves
Using the same yarn color throughout, make a back and two sleeves as given for the raglan sweater on page 34.

Right front
Cast on 11 sts.
Row 1 (RS): K3, [p1, k1] to end.
Row 2: P1, [k1, p1] 4 times, k2.
Row 3: Knit.
Row 4: Purl to last 2 sts, k2.
Repeat last 2 rows nine times more.
Place marker at beginning and end of row.
Row 23: Knit to last 4 sts, k2tog, k2. (10 sts)
Row 24: As row 4.
Repeat last 2 rows twice more. (6 sts)
Do not bind off; slip stitches onto spare needle or stitch holder.

Left front
Cast on 11 sts.
Row 1 (RS): [K1, p1] 4 times, k3.
Row 2: K2, [p1, k1] 4 times, p1.
Row 3: Knit.
Row 4: K2, purl to end.
Repeat last 2 rows nine times more.
Place marker at beginning and end of row.
Row 23: K2, k2togtbl, knit to end.
Row 24: As row 4.
Repeat last 2 rows twice more. (6 sts)
Do not bind off; slip stitches onto spare needle or stitch holder.

Neckband

With RS facing, slip pieces onto left-hand needle in following sequence: right front, sleeve, back, sleeve, left front. (33 sts)

Row 1 (RS): K5, k2tog, k3, k2tog, k9, k2tog, k3, k2tog, k5. (29 sts)

Row 2: Knit.

Row 3: K1, m1, knit to last st, m1, k1. (31 sts)

Row 4: As row 3. (33 sts)

Bind off.

Finishing

Weave in loose ends. Block and press if required. Using mattress stitch, sew up the raglan seams of body and sleeves between markers. Sew up side seams and sleeves.

Garter stitch variation

Make a jacket with a garter stitch welt in place of 1 x 1 rib as follows:

Work as described above, but replace rows 1 and 2 of each piece with 4 rows of garter stitch (knit every row). Note that each piece will be 2 rows longer in total.

Pocket top (make 2)

Cast on 7 sts.

Work 3 rows in garter stitch.

Bind off.

Finish as above, then pin and stitch pocket tops onto front panels. Fold lapels onto RS and catch down.

Coat

Make a double-breasted flared coat for a casual night out or a single-breasted coat with straight sides for a more formal look.

Materials

9 x 12in (23 x 30cm) sheet of felt fabric
Sharp sewing needle and matching thread

Instructions

Using the templates on pages 130–131, cut out back, two fronts, two sleeves, and collar from felt fabric. Make sure that you use the correct templates for the style of coat you are making.

Joining the pieces

With RS together and using ¼in (5mm) seam allowance and backstitch, pin and sew shoulders. Pin sleeves into position, aligning center of sleeves with shoulder seams, and sew together.

Pin and sew side seams, then pin and sew sleeve seams, leaving about ⅜–¾in (1–2cm) unsewn at the wrist to make it easier to slip the doll's hand through. Turn RS out and press with steam iron.

Collar and pockets

Fold collar in half and press. Align center of collar with center of back neck, then pin and stitch into position.

If you want to add pockets, cut out two 1in (2.5cm) squares of felt and sew onto front panels.

YOUR KNITTED
BOYFRIEND'S
FAVORITE MOVIES

1. X Men: Woolverine

2. In the Loop

3. The Whole Nine Yards

4. Cast Away

5. The Dark Knit

Accessories

Add some additional bling to your boyfriend's look.
Make him look less like a sight for sore eyes ...
and give him a pair of trendy glasses or bow tie!

Materials

Long tie
1³/₈ x 6³/₄in (3.5 x 17cm) strip of fabric
Sharp sewing needle and matching thread
Press stud

Bow tie
2in (5cm) length of 1¹/₂in (4cm) wide
ribbon
Sharp sewing needle and matching thread
5¹/₂in (14cm) cord elastic

Boots and gloves
Sport-weight yarn in color of your choice
Pair of size 3 (3.25mm) knitting needles
Tapestry needle

Glasses
Reel of Scientific Wire Company
silver-plated craft wire, or color of
your choice, 0.2mm thick

Note: Look through the boyfriends
chapter for lots more accessory ideas.

Instructions

Long tie
Following illustrations on page 131, start
by folding over ¹/₄in (5mm) lengthways
on left-hand side of fabric and press with
steam iron. Fold over ³/₈in (1cm) on right-
hand side of fabric, then fold again to
create a strip approx ³/₈in (1cm) wide. Sew
seam using hem stitch. Using a knitting
needle point or similar tool, tuck in open
ends of fabric strip and sew together.
Using illustrations as a guide, fold knot at
top to create tie effect. Sew one half of
press stud to WS of knot. Sew other half
of press stud to doll at center front of
neckline. Press the tie onto the doll.

Bow tie
Fold ribbon into three sections, like an
envelope. Work a few stitches at one edge
to secure, then run thread through ribbon
to other edge and work a few stitches to
secure. Squeeze center together to create
a bow tie shape and work a few stitches
to secure.

Place center of cord elastic horizontally across WS of bow tie and stitch into position. Knot the ends of the elastic and slip over doll's head.

Boots (make 2)

Cast on 17 sts.
Knit 3 rows.
Starting and ending with a purl row, work 5 rows in stockinette stitch.
Row 9 (RS): K1, m1, k6, m1, k3, m1, k6, m1, k1. (21 sts)
Row 10: Purl.
Row 11: K9, m1, k3, m1, k9. (23 sts)
Row 12: Purl.
Shape toe as follows:
Row 13: K10, m1, k3, m1, k8, turn.
Row 14: Slip 1, p20, turn.
Row 15: Slip 1, k8, m1, k3, m1, k7, turn.
Row 16: Slip 1, p18, turn.
Row 17: Slip 1, k7, m1, k3, m1, k6, turn.
Row 18: Slip 1, p16, turn.
Row 19: Slip 1, knit to end.
Row 20: P12, p2tog, p1, p2tog, p12. (27 sts)
Bind off. Fold bound-off edge in half and sew together. Slip boot onto doll and sew back seam.

Gloves (make 2)

Cast on 12 sts.
Starting with a knit row, work 8 rows in stockinette stitch.
Row 9 (RS): K4, k2togtbl, k2tog, knit to end. (10 sts)
Row 10: Purl.
Row 11: K3, k2togtbl, k2tog, knit to end. (8 sts)
Row 12: Purl.

Break off yarn, thread through stitches on needle and pull tight, then use yarn tail to sew side seam.

Glasses

Wrap craft wire approx 10 times around two fingers. Break off, leaving a good length. Twist the loop of wire in half to make a figure-of-8, then wrap the end of the wire around the center to create bridge for nose. Cut another length of wire from reel and wrap it around frame of each lens to help hold the frames together. Insert a large knitting needle or similar tool into each circular lens to help refine shape. Alternatively, bend the wire lenses into desired shape. Stitch into position on the doll's face.

45

The
boyfriends

Unravel Your Boyfriend

Sports Fan

Sports Star

Your man lives, breathes, and wears sport. He loves watching other guys throw, hit, or kick a ball around. Sport is his life. Join him glued to the sports channel or at a game, and you'll soon learn about the offside rule, whether you want to or not. Be ready to cheer when his team wins, and commiserate when it loses. Put your name and number on his T-shirt and your heart on his sleeve.

This guy's buff, ripped, athletic, and cute, with a knitted head start on the average boyfriend physique, since working out is part of the job description. As his girlfriend, you'll spend much of your time watching from the sidelines, while he takes the praise and prizes, but only you will get to knit him a trophy of your own design and have 'abs'-olute control.

Favorite movie: *Big Fan*
Favorite expression: Are you blind, ref?!
Never say to him: It's only a game

Favorite sport: Sport
Favorite expression: Want to see some action?

Surfer Dude

Artist

Surfer dudes are cool dudes. They love the marine scene: riding big waves, man versus sea, with salt in their unkempt hair (blonder than yours) and trendy knitted board shorts. Join your surfer by the ocean, or you won't see much of him unless you both get a city job! But being in a close-knit relationship with this guy will mean life's a beach after all and you can reach point break together.

Sensitive, imaginative, visual, temperamental, artists have been taking selfies for years–they just have to wait for the paint to dry. A brush with this guy may leave you in emotional knots, but the experience is bound to be colorful. His moods may be hard to palette at times, but his art is in the right place.

Favorite (Van Gogh) expression: I'm (not) all ears to your problems
Favorite song: "It's Not About The Monet"
Never say to him: My kid sister did one like that

Favorite expression: Surf's up
Second favorite expression: I'm getting barreled
Favorite chat-up line: You're so hot the sun is jealous

Rock Star

Hip-hop Guy

This guy is music to your ears and his own, with a backstage pass straight to knitted boyfriend heaven. Cool and hip, he parties hard all night–you will get to go to some neat venues and meet some badass dudes, but you'll have to make do with less beauty sleep, fight off the fans, and get a matching wardrobe. Knitting rocks, man.

Gangsta or rapper, bro or homie, whichever hip-hop guy is the one for you, you got to work your booty if you want to be Kim to his Kanye. A boyfriend with attitude, you don't disrespect a guy with a hoodie and saggy pants, but a winning way with words. Bust some knitting balls together!

Favorite movie: *This Is Spinal Tap*
Favorite song: "Je Suis Un Rock Star"
Never say to him: I love you, yarn, yarn, yarn

Favorite dance move: Throwing great body popping shapes
Hobbies: Turntablism, breaking and MCing

Outdoorsman

Astronaut

He loves to travel and go where no knitted man has gone before. Mountains, jungles, deserts: he'll chart them all. Good with a compass, and hot on survival skills, he'll seduce you with many a yarn about his adventures around the campfire. Stitch along for the ride if you're brave enough.

This guy is out of the world, literally. You may not get to see him for months but he will have some great photographs to show you and you could soon both be head over heels. With an astronaut boyfriend the sky's definitely not the limit, but don't let him out of your sight—in space no one can see you unravel.

Favorite dance move: Moonwalk
Favorite expression: You're out of this world
Favorite chat-up line: May the fourth row be with you

Favorite movie: *Jurassic Park*
Hobbies: Checking out noises in the attic and appearing in T-rex themed weddings

Doctor

Businessman

The doctor is cute and kind. Great to have around in an emergency, he'll soon cure any heartache, though if you drop a stitch, he could be the cause of it. A knit-ural in the caring department, your mum will love him and you should feel as safe in his hands as he is in yours. A purl among men...

The professional about town, he takes his job seriously and works hard, but parties hard too. Knit this executive toy if you want a guy who's a team player with a win-win attitude to blue-sky thinking and a big bank balance. When office politics make him hot under the collar, he will let off steam by whisking you away to the south of France in his Lexus.

Favorite dance move: Dad dancing
Hobbies: Keeping his knitted finger on the pulse

Favorite dance move: The hustle
Favorite movie: *The Wolf of Wall Street*

Fireman

Skateboarder

Who doesn't like a man in uniform? A firefighter boyfriend is hot, hot, hot—24/7! Rescuing kittens from trees, helping small boys remove their heads from between railings, he is never off duty and will light your fire but put out others. Knit a fireman and he'll be at your side through thick and thin wool.

Always on the move, a skater boy comes with a warning. Get a skateboard or your relationship will be termi-knitted. Stick with him and he'll turn you head over heels as he hurtles down a half-pipe and shoots off a ramp with twists. You will need to keep fit to keep up with this knitted guy.

Favorite movie: *Top Gun*
Favorite expression: Ollie, Nollie, Ollie North

Favorite dance move:
Fireman Carry
Favorite song: "Light my Fire"

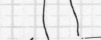

Nerd

Superhero

Knit this dream screen lover and you'll never need to call in tech support. With the right password you can lure him out of his webcave and swap stories about downloads and upgrades. His world may be virtual but you can navigate his operating system and hack into his personal program.

Not your average kind of guy, this is one boyfriend who is big on benefits. Life will be action-packed and you'll be fighting the battle of good versus evil every day. His wardrobe may not vary—even on dress-down Fridays—but who cares when he looks so cute flying through the air or scampering up the side of buildings. Just don't try to make him wear his underwear on the inside.

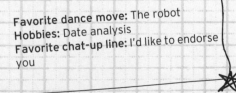

Favorite dance move: The robot
Hobbies: Date analysis
Favorite chat-up line: I'd like to endorse you

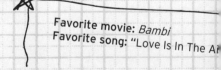

Favorite movie: *Bambi*
Favorite song: "Love Is In The Ai[r]"

Hipster

Is Your Knitted Boyfriend for Real?

- Does he wear the same expression all the time?

- Is he about 12in (30cm) tall?

- Does he squeeze easily?

- Is he the soft, silent type?

- Does he wear the same pants every day?

If you've ticked 0-1 boxes he's an impostor.
1-2 boxes he's stringing you along.
5 boxes he's the real knitted deal.

Your guy thinks and stands (and dances) outside the box. He wears vintage clothes with skinny jeans, ironic eyewear, ironic statement T-shirts, ironic shoes, and ironic piercings. From independent labels to independent thinking, he will be sew into you that he will never want to consciously uncouple. Follow knitted suit, sit on pavements or ride a strange bike, and you can be joined at the hipsters.

Favorite dance move: Hipster dancing with retro moves
Favorite expression: Totally deck
Most likely to say: I only like their early stuff

Sports Fan

Home or away, his team jersey is always the preferred outfit du jour. Keep him cool and warm while he is watching his team.

Materials

Doll

Rowan Cotton Glacé (100% cotton; approx 125yds/115m per 50g ball):
1 ball in 725 Ecru (A)
1 ball in 850 Cobalt (C)
1 ball in 829 Twilight (D)
Rowan Tweed (100% wool; approx 129yds/118m per 50g ball):
1 ball in 591 Burnsall (B)
Rowan Pure Wool DK (100% super wash wool; approx 142yds/130m per 50g ball):
1 ball in 018 Earth (E)
Pair of size 3 (3.25mm) knitting needles
Polyester toy stuffing
Tapestry and embroidery needles
Black and red embroidery thread for facial features
Crochet hook

Jeans

Old jeans or 10in (25cm) square of denim fabric
Sharp sewing needle and white and orange thread

Rowan Handknit Cotton (100% cotton; approx 93yds/85m per 50g ball):
1 ball in 353 Violet (F)
1 ball in 263 Bleached (G)
1 ball in 251 Rosso (H)
Extra size 3 (3.25mm) knitting needle for three-needle bind-off
6in (15cm) square of white felt fabric
Sharp sewing needle and white thread

Football

Patons 100% Cotton DK (100% cotton; approx 230yds/210m per 100g ball):
1 ball in 2723 Nectarine (J)
Polyester toy stuffing
Short length of white yarn

Instructions

Doll

Make a basic doll with a tall and slim body shape (page 10) and a messy and tousled hairstyle (page 24), using yarn colors as follows:

Legs: Yarn B, working final row (row 36) of each leg as knit instead of purl to define bottom hem of trousers.

Feet: Yarn D.

Body and head: Use yarn C from pick-up row to end of row 32 of body, then break off C and join in A. Use yarn A to complete neck and head.

Arms and hands: Use yarn C from cast-on to end of row 20 of arms, then break off C and join in A. Use yarn A to complete arms and hands.

Soles: Yarn D.

Hair: Yarn E.

Eyebrows: Split a length of yarn E down to 2 strands and use this to add eyebrows in backstitch.

Jeans

Make a pair of jeans (page 30) and dress the doll. This boyfriend also has knitted trousers as part of the basic doll if you don't want to make the jeans.

Football shirt
Back

Using F, cast on 27 sts.
Knit 2 rows.

Row 3 (RS): Knit.
Row 4: K3, purl to last 3 sts, k3.
Repeat last 2 rows once more.
Starting with a knit row, work 22 rows in stockinette stitch.
Without breaking off F, join in G.
Using G, knit 2 rows.
Break off G and continue in F.
Starting with a knit row, work 12 rows in stockinette stitch.
Next row: K7, bind off 13 sts, knit to last 7 sts.
Slip both sets of 7 sts onto spare needle or stitch holder.

Front

Work first 30 rows as given for Back (to end of white stripe).
Break off G and continue in F.
Shape each side of neck separately as follows:
Row 31 (RS): K13, k2tog, knit to end. (26 sts)
Next row: P11, k2, turn and work on these 13 sts only to shape right side of neck.
Next row: K2, k2togtbl, knit to end. (12 sts)
Next row: Purl to last 4 sts, p2togtbl, k2. (11 sts)
Repeat last 2 rows twice more. (7 sts)
Next row: Knit.
Next row: Purl to last 2 sts, k2.
Repeat last 2 rows twice more.
Slip these 7 sts onto spare needle or stitch holder and break off yarn, leaving enough to bind off.
With WS facing, rejoin F to remaining

13 sts to shape left side of neck.
Next row: K2, purl to end.
Next row: Knit to last 4 sts, k2tog, k2. (12 sts)
Next row: K2, p2tog, purl to end. (11 sts)
Repeat last 2 rows twice more. (7 sts)
Next row: Knit.
Next row: K2, purl to end.
Repeat last 2 rows twice more.
Slip these 7 sts onto spare needle or stitch holder and break off yarn, leaving enough to bind off.
Slip both sets of 7 sts from front of shirt onto one needle and both sets of 7 sts from back of shirt onto another needle. With RS together and the 7 sts of left and right shoulders aligned, bind off each pair of 7 sts together using three-needle bind-off method to join shoulders.

Sleeves (make 2)

Using F, cast on 22 sts.
Knit 2 rows.
Work stripes as follows:
Using H, knit 2 rows.
Using F and starting with a knit row, work 6 rows in stockinette stitch.
Using G, knit 2 rows.
Using F, knit 1 row.
Bind off.

Finishing

Weave in loose ends. Block and press if required. With RS facing, pin center top of sleeves to shoulder seams of shirt. Using mattress stitch, sew sleeves to shirt, making sure that white stripe on sleeves aligns with stripe on shirt. Sew up side seams and sleeves, again making sure that all stripes align.
Using template on page 139, cut numbers out of white felt. Pin and stitch numbers to front and back of shirt.

Football

Using J, cast on 6 sts.
Row 1 (WS): Purl.
Row 2: K2, [m1, k1] to end. (10 sts)
Row 3: Purl.
Row 4: K2, [m1, k2] to end. (14 sts)
Row 5: [P3, m1] to last 2 sts, k2. (18 sts)
Row 6: K2, [m1, k4] to last 4 sts, m1, knit to end. (22 sts)
Starting and ending with a purl row, work 11 rows in stockinette stitch.
Row 18: K2, [k2tog, k3] to end. (18 sts)
Row 19: P2, [p2tog, p2] to last 3 sts, p2tog, p1. (14 sts)
Row 20: K1, [k2tog, k1] to last st, k1. (10 sts)
Row 21: Purl.
Row 22: K1, [k2tog] to end.
Row 23: Purl.
Break off yarn, leaving long enough length to sew up. Thread yarn through stitches on needle and pull tight.

Finishing

With RS facing and using mattress stitch, sew halfway along seam, insert stuffing and then complete the seam. Using picture as a guide, add some white stitching along the seam.

Surfer Dude

The only thing this totally awesome boyfriend needs is radical surf as bodacious as his brightly colored board shorts.

Materials

Doll and shorts

Rowan Pure Wool DK (100% super wash wool; approx 142yds/130m per 50g ball):
  1 ball in 054 Tan (A)
Rowan Fine Tweed (100% wool; approx 98yds/90m per 25g ball):
  1 ball in 360 Arncliffe (B)
Rowan Big Wool (100% merino wool; approx 87yds/80m per 100g ball):
  1 ball in 048 Linen (C)
Pair of size 3 (3.25mm) knitting needles
Polyester toy stuffing
Tapestry and embroidery needles
Black and red embroidery thread for facial features
Two 5½in (14cm) squares of brightly colored cotton fabric
8in (20cm) cord elastic
Sharp sewing needle and thread to match fabric (and felt colors listed right if making surfboard)

Surfboard

3¼ x 10in (8 x 25cm) piece of cardboard for template
9 x 12in (23 x 30cm) sheets of white and yellow felt fabric
⅜ x 3¼in (1 x 8cm) strip of black felt fabric
Press stud
9in (23cm) length of black sport-weight yarn

Knit on, dude!

Instructions

Doll

Make a basic doll with a short and stocky body shape (page 10) and a dreadlocks hairstyle (page 22), using yarn colors as follows:

Doll: Yarn A.

Hair: Use yarn B for the hair base and yarn C for the dreadlocks.

Shorts

Dress the doll in a pair of brightly colored beach shorts (page 32).

Surfboard
Board

Using template on page 133, cut a surfboard template from cardboard. Place cardboard template on white felt fabric and draw around it, adding 1/4in (5mm) extra all around. Cut around line to make front panel, then repeat for back panel.

Cut a 3/4in (2cm) wide strip of yellow felt for the contrast stripe. Pin it along center of front panel, trim to match top point of board and then sew in place using backstitch.

Sandwich the cardboard template between front and back panels and pin around outer edge. Sew layers together, leaving bottom section open for attaching ankle strap cord.

Strap and cord

Sew one half of press stud to RH side of black felt strip. Turn felt strip over so that press stud is on the LH side facing down. Sew other half of press stud to RH side. Sew length of black yarn to center of ankle strap.

Use a tapestry needle to make a hole 3/4in (2cm) up from bottom edge of surfboard, through center of yellow strip. Use a knitting needle or similar tool to widen the hole. Thread the needle with the loose end of black yarn and thread it through the hole. Tie a knot to secure. Sew along the bottom edge of the board.

Attach ankle strap around left ankle of doll.

THE PURLFECT BOYFRIEND

1. Never cancels date night for a guys' night out.

2. Always washes the dishes after a romantic meal cooked by you (or better still him).

3. Isn't thinner than you and doesn't have better hair or skin.

4. Would rather go shopping with you than play on his X-box.

5. Is brave with insects and wildlife, including spiders, mice, bears, and crocodiles.

6. Doesn't 'like' other girls' Facebook photos.

7. Regularly asks if you've lost weight.

8. Invites you to meet his friends early on in the relationship.

9. Likes your pet but not as much as you (do).

10. Never calls you by the wrong name – ever.

11. Is a great kisser without giving you beard rash.

12. Sends you good morning and good night texts.

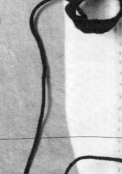

Artist

Constantly covered in bright paint, his clothes clogging up the washing machine, this boyfriend is too busy concentrating on his masterpiece to pay attention to his scruffy attire.

Materials

Doll and outfit

Rowan Cotton Glacé (100% cotton; approx 125yds/115m per 50g ball):
  1 ball in 725 Ecru (A)
  1 ball in 727 Black (B)
  1 ball in 739 Dijon (C)
Rowan Creative Focus Worsted (75% wool, 25% alpaca; approx 220yds/200m per 100g ball):
  1 ball in 500 Ebony (D)
Rowan Felted Tweed DK (50% merino wool, 25% alpaca, 25% viscose; approx 191yds/175m per 50g ball):
  1 ball in 159 Carbon (E)
Rowan Pure Wool 4ply (100% super wash wool; approx 174yds/160m per 50g ball):
  1 ball in 404 Black (F)
Pair of size 3 (3.25mm) knitting needles
Polyester toy stuffing
Tapestry and embroidery needles
Black and red embroidery thread for facial features
Crochet hook

Old T-shirt or 8in (20cm) square of jersey fabric
Sharp sewing needle and thread to match fabric
Acrylic paint in various colors (plus brown for paintbrush below)

Easel

Three bamboo skewers, approx 10in (25cm) long
Two lolly sticks, approx $4^1/4$in (11cm) long
Craft knife, superglue, and Blu-Tack

Canvas

$3^1/2$ x $4^1/2$in (9 x 11.5cm) rectangle of cardboard
$4^1/4$ x $5^1/4$in (11 x 13.5cm) rectangle of white felt fabric

Paintbrush

Short bamboo skewer
Short length of beige yarn
20in (50cm) silver-plated craft wire, 0.2mm thick
Craft knife and superglue

Palette

3¹/₄in (8cm) square of cardboard for template
3¹/₄ x 6¹/₄in (8 x 16cm) rectangle of gray felt fabric
Small scraps of red, yellow, turquoise, and lime felt fabric
Thread to match felt fabrics

Instructions

Doll

Make a basic doll with a short and slim body shape (page 10), a ponytail hairstyle (page 22), and a goatee (page 27), using yarn colors as follows:

Legs: Yarn B, working final row (row 30) of each leg as knit instead of purl to define bottom hem of trousers.
Feet: Yarn C.
Body and head: Yarn A.
Arms and hands: Yarn A.
Soles: Yarn C.
Hair and goatee: Yarn D, with about four strands of yarn E in the ponytail for a gray streak.

Outfit

Make a short- or long-sleeved T-shirt (page 31) and add the finishing touch by spattering it with brightly colored acrylic paint. Dress the doll.

Easel

Glue pointed tips of two skewers together. Insert flat ends of skewers into Blu-Tack so that they stand upright, then allow to dry. Make pencil marks 2³/₄in (7cm) up from base of skewers. Glue a lolly stick across the skewers at the pencil marks, making sure that it is evenly positioned. Allow to dry.
Use a craft knife to trim the second lolly stick to approx 2¹/₂in (6cm) long by cutting off each curved end. Mark the skewers 1³/₄in (4.5cm) down from top. Glue trimmed lolly stick across marked points and allow to dry.
Glue tip of third skewer to back of first two skewers to make a tripod and allow to dry.

Canvas

Place cardboard in center of felt fabric and draw around it. Remove cardboard and cut a ³/₈in (1cm) square from each corner of the felt so that you are left with flaps along each of the four sides. Fold the flaps over and press with a steam iron. Place cardboard on WS of felt fabric, fold over the flaps and stitch each of the corners together.

Paintbrush

Cut a 1½in (4cm) section of bamboo skewer, paint it brown and allow to dry. Wrap the beige yarn around your finger approx 10 times. Remove from finger and wind remaining tail of yarn around base. Fold silver wire in half and wrap it a few times around base of yarn.

Insert painted skewer into wrapped base of yarn and continue wrapping wire around yarn and skewer. Once all the wire has been wrapped around, add a spot of glue to secure and allow to dry. Once dry, trim the yarn to look like the bristles of a paintbrush.

Palette

Using template on page 135, cut a palette template from cardboard. Place cardboard template onto gray felt fabric and draw around it, adding ¼in (5mm) extra all around. Cut around line to make front panel, then repeat for back panel. Cut a few small random shapes of colored felt. Place them on front panel and stitch into position. Sandwich cardboard template between front and back panels, then pin around outer edge. Sew layers together using backstitch.

YOUR KNITTED
BOYFRIEND LOVES
YOU BECAUSE

1. You're a knitphomaniac!

2. He's scared of your pointy sticks!

3. You always have him in stitches!

4. You've got a tight-knit group of friends!

5. You offer many purls of wisdom!

Rock Star

This boyfriend loves his band more than anything.
He sleeps until noon and stays up all night
practicing guitar solos. All the cool dudes are
rocking wool these days, so let your rock star's
new jacket take center stage at his next gig.

Knitting is the new
rock and roll

Materials

Doll and jacket

Rowan Cotton Glacé (100% cotton; approx 125yds/115m per 50g ball):
   1 ball in 730 Oyster (A)
   1 ball in 739 Dijon (B)
   1 ball in 727 Black (C)
Rowan Summer Tweed (70% silk, 30% cotton; approx 131yds/120m per 50g ball):
   1 ball in 530 Toast (D)
Rowan Felted Tweed DK (50% merino wool, 25% alpaca, 25% viscose; approx 191yds/175m per 50g ball):
   1 ball in 154 Ginger (E)
   1 ball in 172 Ancient (F)
Pair of size 3 (3.25mm) knitting needles
Polyester toy stuffing
Tapestry and embroidery needles
Blue and red embroidery thread for facial features

Jeans

Old jeans or 10in (25cm) square of denim fabric
Sharp sewing needle and white and orange thread

Guitar

6in (15cm) square of green felt fabric
2 x 4in (5 x 10cm) piece of black felt fabric
Small pieces of gray and white felt fabric
Sharp sewing needle and thread to match felt colors

Instructions

Doll

Make a basic doll with a short and stocky body shape (page 10) and a 1950s quiff hairstyle (page 20), using yarn colors as follows:

Legs: Yarn B, working final row (row 30) of each leg as knit instead of purl to define bottom hem of trousers.

Feet: Yarn D.

Body and head: Use yarn C from pick-up row to end of row 26 of body, then break off C and join in A. Use yarn A to complete neck and head.

Arms and hands: Use yarn C from cast-on to end of row 26 of arms, then break off C and join in A. Use yarn A to work hands.

Soles: Yarn D.

Hair: Yarn E.

Outfit

Using F, make a knitted jacket (page 40) following the instructions for the garter stitch variation.

Make a pair of jeans (page 30) and dress the doll. This boyfriend also has trousers knitted as part of the basic doll if you don't want to make the jeans.

Guitar

Using templates on page 131, cut the guitar pieces from felt fabric using colors indicated. Sew front and back of guitar neck together (black felt). Pin and sew front and back of guitar body together (green felt), sandwiching end of neck between the layers. Sandwich other end of neck between the two head stock pieces (green felt). Pin and sew other sections to guitar using the photograph as a guide.

YOUR KNITTED BOYFRIEND'S FAVORITE ARTISTS

1. Slipknot

2. The Cardigans

3. Rage Against the Sewing Machine

4. Purl Jam

5. Knitney Spears

Hip-Hop Guy

This boyfriend's gonna swag it out 'cos he's the flyest playa on the block. You'll need to speak hip hop to be joined at the hip or he'll hop.

Materials

Doll

Rowan British Sheep Breeds DK Undyed (100% British wool; approx 131yds/120m per 50g ball):
  1 ball in 781 Brown Bluefaced Leicester (A)
Rowan Felted Tweed DK (50% merino wool, 25% alpaca, 25% viscose; approx 191yds/175m per 50g ball):
  1 ball in 170 Seafarer (B)
Patons 100% Cotton DK (100% cotton; approx 230yds/210m per 100g ball):
  1 ball in 2721 Orchard (C)
  1 ball in 2691 White (D)
  1 ball in 2712 Black (E)
Pair of size 3 (3.25mm) knitting needles
Polyester toy stuffing
Tapestry and embroidery needles
Black and red embroidery thread for facial features, plus purple thread for shoelaces
Crochet hook

Outfit

Old jeans or two 8in (20cm) squares of denim fabric
Old T-shirt or 8in (20cm) square of jersey fabric
Leftover yarn E from making the doll
2in (5cm) square of white felt fabric
Sharp sewing needle and thread to match fabric and felt colors

Headphones

Leftover yarn D from making the doll
Two size 1/2 (2.5mm) double-pointed needles for working i-cord
2³/₄in (7cm) memory wire
2in (5cm) square of orange felt fabric

Boombox

8in (20cm) square of black felt fabric
2¹/₂in (6cm) square each of dark gray and light gray felt fabric
Scraps of red, yellow, and turquoise felt fabric
Empty matchbox, approx 3¹/₄ x 1³/₄in (8 x 4.5cm)
Sharp sewing needle and thread to match felt colors

Instructions

Doll

Make a basic doll with a tall and slim body shape (page 10) and a cornrows hairstyle (page 24), using yarn colors as follows:

Legs: Yarn B, working final row (row 36) of each leg as knit instead of purl to define bottom hem of trousers.
Feet: Yarn C.
Body and head: Yarn A.
Arms and hands: Yarn A.
Soles: Yarn D.
Hair: Yarn E.
Shoelaces: Use purple thread to embroider a few straight stitches across top of shoes.

Baggy jeans

Using template on page 137, make a pair of baggy jeans using the instructions given for the Skateboarder boyfriend on page 90, but don't hem the legs or pinch in the fabric at the sides.

After sewing the waistband, turn the jeans RS out and place on the doll. Fold over the bottom of each leg for turn-ups. Pinch the fabric at the back of each leg to gather in the fabric at the waistband, then pin and sew in place.

This boyfriend also has trousers knitted as part of the basic doll if you don't want to make the jeans, or you could dress him in a pair of slim-fit jeans if you prefer (page 30).

T-shirt

Using templates on page 136, cut out back, front, and two sleeves from an old T-shirt using the existing hem for your hem on each piece. If using jersey fabric, add an extra hemming allowance to the bottom of each piece– 1½in (4cm) on front and back, and ¾in (2cm) on each sleeve–and then hem and sew together as described on page 31.

Cap

Using E, cast on 32 sts.
Row 1: Knit to end.
Row 2: P28, k4.
Row 3: Bind off 4 sts, knit to end. (28 sts)
Starting and ending with a purl row, work 5 rows in stockinette stitch.
Row 9: K1, m1, knit to last st, m1, k1. (30 sts)
Row 10: P1, m1, purl to last st, m1, p1. (32 sts)
Row 11: K4, *k2tog, k3, rep from * to 3 sts, k2tog, k1. (26 sts)
Row 12: P1, *p2tog, p2 rep from * to last st, p1. (20 sts)
Row 13: K2, *k2tog, k1, rep from * to end. (14 sts)
Row 14: P1, * p2tog, rep from * to last st, p1. (8 sts)
Break off yarn leaving long enough length to thread through stitches on needle and pull tight and secure.

Top brim

With RS facing, miss 8 sts then pick up 12 sts along cast-on edge.

Knit to end.
Row 2: K2togtbl, knit to last 2 sts, k2tog.
Row 3: K2togtbl, knit to 2 sts, k2tog.
Row 4: Knit to end.
Row 5: Sl1, k2tog psso, bind off until 3 sts remain on left-hand needle, k3tog, bind off.

Bottom brim section
Using template on page 137, cut out white felt section.
Pin and stitch into place.

Headphones
Headband
Using double-pointed needles and E, cast on 4 sts and work i-cord as follows:
Row 1: Knit.
Do not turn; slide the stitches to other end of needle.
Pull yarn tightly across back of work and knit one more row.
Repeat until 28 rows have been worked, then bind off.

Cans (make 2)
Using double-pointed needles, cast on 20 sts.
Knit 4 rows.
Row 5 (RS): K2, [k2tog, k1] to end. (14 sts)
Row 6: Purl.
Row 7: K1, [k2tog] to last st, k1. (8 sts)
Break off yarn and thread through stitches on needle. Pull tight and sew side seam.

Finishing
Insert memory wire through the headband i-cord with approx $^3/_8$in (1cm) protruding at each end. Insert stuffing into each of the cans, then insert the ends of the headband wire into the cans. Add more stuffing if required. Cut out two circles from orange felt fabric to match the circumference of the cans. Pin and sew into position.

Boombox
Using the template on page 136, cut the main ghetto blaster piece from black felt fabric. Cut two small circles from light gray and two larger circles from dark gray felt fabric. Place a light gray circle onto each dark gray circle, making sure they are centered, and stitch into position. Sew the gray circles onto the black felt fabric, approx $^3/_4$in (2cm) in from each side edge and $1^1/_4$in (3cm) down from the top. Cut small rectangles of turquoise, red, and yellow felt fabric. Using the photograph as a guide, sew them above the gray circles. Wrap the black felt around the matchbox, folding the flaps into place around it, then pin and sew in place.
Cut a $^3/_8$ x $3^1/_4$in (1 x 8cm) strip of black felt fabric and pin and stitch into position for the handle.

Knit One, Pull One

MAKE A NEW MATCH
Mix and match the dolls, hairstyles, and clothes to make new boyfriends.
1. DJ (Your Skateboarder boyfriend could wear the Artist's T-shirt and the Hip-hop Guy's headphones)
2. Philosopher (Put the Artist in the Nerd's gear)
3. Boyband Heartthrob (Put a beardless Hipster in a hoodie or smart jacket)
4. Glastonbury & Coachella Man (The Artist in the Surfer Dude's shorts)
5. Multimillionaire (How about the Businessman in the Astronaut's helmet?)

GET KNOTTED, KNIT NOT
Don't knit these guys or they may needle you big time!
1. Yoga Dude: he prefers downward dog to getting on with you and yours.
2. Casual Man: he's just not that into you.
3. Smooth Operator: he has all the chat but none of the commitment.
4. Adrenaline Junkie: he surfs, skydives, runs with the bulls, never relaxes.
5. Workaholic: you will have to share his life with his Android.

STITCHED UP OR HITCHED UP
He is boyfriend material if:
1. He remembers facts and details and things about you.
2. He makes you laugh.
3. He gets on well with his family.
4. He will drop everything if you need him.
5. He has goals and dreams and pursues them.

HOW TO TIE UP YOUR BOYFRIEND IN KNOTS
1. Book a surprise break in a place you know he's always wanted to go to.
2. Tell him you are knitting a scarf in his team's colors.
3. Take him his favorite dish to work when he's working late.
4. Tell him he looks cool—at least twice a week.
5. Buy two tickets for something he likes and you hate—like a football game or an obscure rapper's gig.

'I knit,
therefore I am'

Outdoorsman

Adventurous boyfriends usually turn up at your door covered in mud, dust, and cobwebs. But if your boyfriend has a habit of dashing off to some exotic, faraway island, you might as well make him look dashing too, especially if he takes you with him!

Materials

Doll and outfit

Rowan Pure Wool DK (100% super wash wool; approx 142yds/130m per 50g ball):
    1 ball in 054 Tan (A)
    1 ball in 018 Earth (B)
Rowan Cotton Glacé (100% cotton; approx 125yds/115m per 50g ball):
    1 ball in 739 Dijon (C)
    1 ball in 727 Black (D)
Rowan Tweed (100% wool; approx 129yds/118m per 50g ball):
    1 ball in 589 Hubberholme (E)
Anchor Tapestry wool (100% wool; approx 11yd (10m) per skein):
    1 skein in 9314 (F)
Pair of size 3 (3.25mm) knitting needles
Polyester toy stuffing
Tapestry and embroidery needles
Black and red embroidery thread for facial features

Old pair of khaki green army trousers or 16in (40cm) square of utility-weight polycotton khaki fabric
Press stud
4in (10cm) square of black felt fabric for hat
Sharp sewing needle and thread to match fabric and felt colors (including for items below)

Map

4in (10cm) squares of felt fabric in pale blue (A), mid-blue (B), beige (C), green (D), and oatmeal (E)
Blue and ochre embroidery thread

Compass

2in (5cm) square of black felt fabric
¾in (2cm) square of gray felt fabric
Small amount of red and white embroidery thread

Instructions

Doll

Make a basic doll with a tall and stocky body shape (page 10), a shoulder-length hairstyle (page 21) and a mustache and sideburns (page 27), using yarn colors as follows:

Legs: Yarn A.
Feet: Yarn D.
Body and head: Use yarn C from cast-on to end of row 32 of body, then break off C and join in A. Use yarn A to complete neck and head.
Arms and hands: Use yarn C from cast-on to end of row 6 or arms, then break off C and join in A. Use yarn A to complete arms and hands.
Soles: Yarn D.
Hair: Yarn B.

Outfit

Socks (make 2)

Using F, cast on 17 sts.
Row 1: K1, [p1, k1] to end.
Row 2: P1, [k1, p1] to end.
Row 3: As row 1.
Bind off.
Sew short edges together and slip onto doll's ankles.

Jacket and shorts

Using E, make a knitted jacket following the main pattern instructions (page 40). Make a pair of tailored shorts using khaki fabric (page 33). Dress the doll.

Hat

Crown

Using D, cast on 8 sts.
Row 1 (WS): Purl.
Row 2 (RS): Knit into front and back of each st. (16 sts)
Row 3: Purl.
Row 4: As row 2. (32 sts)
Starting and ending with a purl row, work 9 rows in stockinette stitch.
Bind off.
Sew up side seam, leaving cast-on edge open.
Turn hat WS out, flatten with side seam to the left so that cast-on edge stitches are together at the top and then sew along the top using backstitch. This will help give the hat its shape.
Weave in all loose ends.

Brim

Using template on page 135, cut a circular ring from black felt fabric. Snip small cuts around inside of ring as marked on template. Fold snips upward and place around bound-off edge of knitted section. Pin and sew into position using backstitch.
Fold up sides of brim, making sure that knitted seam is to the front. Pin and catch each side in place with a few stitches. Press top of front seam with fingers to help create shape of hat.

Binoculars

Using D, cast on 24 sts.

Knit 2 rows.

Row 3 (RS): K1, k2togtbl, k7, k2togtbl, k2tog, k7, k2tog, k1. (20 sts)

Starting and ending with a purl row, work 3 rows in stockinette stitch.

Row 7: K1, k2togtbl, k5, k2togtbl, k2tog, k5, k2tog, k1. (16 sts)

Starting with a purl row, work 2 rows in stockinette stitch.

Bind off.

Finishing

With WS facing, lay flat and roll RH edge to center to form first lens. Sew into place, then repeat with LH edge. Weave in all loose ends. To make cord for hanging binoculars around doll's neck, cut a 10in (25cm) length of yarn and attach ends inside bound-off edges. Help to refine the shape if necessary by inserting a large knitting needle into each lens piece from cast-on edge.

Behind every great knitter is a great knitted boyfriend

Map

Using templates on page 135, cut map sections from felt fabric in colors indicated. Place section B onto section A, aligning the edge of B with the dotted line marked on A. Pin and stitch into position using backstitch. Repeat this process to add sections C and D.

Mark six horizontal lines approx $^5/_{16}$in (7mm) apart on map. Stitch along these lines using blue thread and backstitch. Repeat to add vertical lines. Embroider contour lines on the green section using ochre thread. Sew in all loose ends. Trim remaining square of felt fabric to match map, then sew together around the edge using backstitch.

Compass

Cut two 2 x $^3/_4$ x 1in (2.5cm) rectangles of black felt fabric. Using short edge as top of compass, embroider a white capital N at center top edge of first black rectangle.

Cut a $^3/_8$in (1cm) circle from gray felt fabric and stitch to black rectangle below the N. Embroider a two-color compass needle vertically across the gray circle, with a red satin stitch pointing north and a white satin stitch pointing south. Place second rectangle of black felt underneath and sew together around outer edge using backstitch.

Astronaut

This boyfriend is forever looking at the stars contemplating life, the universe, and everything. Or he just likes playing with rockets. Either way, he'll need the perfect outfit when zooming through space.

Materials

Rowan Cotton Glacé (100% cotton; approx 125yds/115m per 50g ball):
 1 ball in 843 Toffee (A)
 1 ball in 831 Dawn Grey (B)
 1 ball in 726 Bleached (C)
Rowan Creative Focus Worsted (75% wool, 25% alpaca; approx 220yds/200m per 100g ball):
 1 ball in 500 Ebony (D)
Pair of size 3 (3.25mm) knitting needles
Two size 3 (3.25mm) double-pointed needles for working i-cord
Polyester toy stuffing
Tapestry and embroidery needles
Black and red embroidery thread for facial features
20in (50cm) square of white cotton fabric
8in (20cm) squares of white and gray felt fabric
4in (10cm) square of red felt fabric
Scraps of black and blue felt fabric
Sharp sewing needle and thread to match fabric and felt colors
5 press studs
Reel of Scientific Wire Company silver-plated craft wire, 0.2mm thick
8in (20cm) cord elastic
Clear plastic round yoghurt pot

Instructions

Doll
Make a basic doll with a short and slim body shape (page 10) and an Afro hairstyle (page 19), using yarn colors as follows:
Doll: Yarn A.
Hair: Yarn D.

Gloves and boots
Using B, make a pair of gloves and boots (page 45).

Space suit
Using templates on page 133, cut space suit front, back, and two sleeves from white fabric.
With RS together and using ¼in (5mm) seam allowance and backstitch, pin and sew shoulder seams. Pin sleeves into

position, aligning center of sleeves with shoulder seams, and sew in place.

Pin and sew side seams, then sleeve seams and inside leg seams. Fold up ³/₈in (1cm) hem at bottom of each leg and sleeve and sew in place. Turn RS out.

Cut collar and left and right plackets from white felt fabric. Pin and stitch placket to back opening, with narrow strip on left and wider strip on right, making sure that they match up. Pin and stitch collar around neckline. Sew press stud to back opening of collar.

Sew one half of another press stud to front of each sleeve, ¹/₄in (5mm) up from bottom hem and ⁵/₈in (1.5cm) up from sleeve seam. Sew other half of press stud ¹/₄in (5mm) further along from sleeve seam. Cut a ⁵/₁₆ x 3¹/₄in (7mm x 8cm) strip of red felt fabric and sew around middle of each sleeve.

Front panel

Cut a 1³/₈ x 1³/₄in (3.5 x 4.5cm) rectangle from white felt fabric. Cut two ³/₈in (1cm) circles from black felt, plus one red and one blue felt circle slightly smaller than the black. Sew colored circles onto black ones, then stitch onto front panel using picture as a guide. Cut three small rectangles from gray felt and sew onto front panel.

Tube (make 2)

Using double-pointed needles and B, cast on 3 sts and work i-cord as follows:

Row 1: Knit.

Do not turn; slide the stitches to other end of needle.

Pull yarn tightly across back of work and knit one more row.

Repeat until 30 rows have been worked in total. Bind off and weave in loose ends. Sew end of one tube to red felt circle on front panel, and end of second tube to blue circle. Pin and stitch panel to front of space suit.

Helmet

Using C, cast on 32 sts. Knit 2 rows.

Row 3 (RS): Knit.

Row 4: K2, purl to last 2 sts, k2.

Repeat last 2 rows five times more.

Row 15: K7, [k2tog, k5] 3 times, k2tog, k2. (28 sts)

Row 16 and all WS rows: As row 2.

Row 17: K6, [k2tog, k4] 3 times, k2tog, k2. (24 sts)

Row 19: K5, [k2tog, k3] 3 times, k2tog, k2. (20 sts)

Row 21: K4, [k2tog, k2] 3 times, k2tog, k2. (16 sts)

Row 23: K3, [k2tog, k1] 3 times, k2tog, k2. (12 sts)

Row 25: K2, [k2tog] to last 2 sts, k2. (8 sts)

Break off yarn and thread through stitches on needle. Pull tight and secure the end.

Visor

Using template on page 133, cut visor from yoghurt pot. Using sharp needle, punch holes around outer edge of visor, ¹/₄in (5mm) in from edge. Sew knitted section to visor.

Cut a ³/₄in (2cm) wide neckband from gray felt fabric, long enough to go around bottom edge of helmet with small

84

overlap at back. Sew into position.
Sew one half of a press stud to space suit
collar in line with each shoulder seam,
then sew other half of press studs to
inside of helmet neckband to match.

Rocket (make 2)

Use yarn B and craft wire together
throughout, cast on 18 sts.
Starting with a knit row, work 21 rows in
stockinette stitch.
Row 22 (WS): Knit.
Row 23 (RS): K3, [k2togtbl, k2] 3 times,
k2togtbl, k1. (14 sts)
Row 24: Purl.
Row 25: K2, [k2togtbl, k1] 3 times,
k2togtbl, k1. (10 sts)
Row 26: Purl.
Row 27: K1, [k2togtbl] to last st, k1.
(6 sts)
Row 28: Purl.

Break off yarn and wire and thread
through sts on needle, leaving long
enough tail of yarn B to sew side seam.
Tuck tail end of wire into the inside.
Insert stuffing and mold into shape.
Cut two 1¼in (3cm) circles of gray felt
and sew to base of each rocket.

Making backpack
Sew rockets together between base and
row of garter stitch (row 22).
Cut cord elastic in half to make arm
straps. Position the straps on back of
rocket pack toward outer edges. For
each strap, thread tapestry needle with
elastic, insert needle into rocket two
rows below shaping and then bring it
out 1¼in (3cm) further down. Knot ends
of elastic together and tuck knot inside
knitting. Sew the tubes attached to
front panel to back of each rocket,
just above base.

Doctor

Scrub up this boyfriend and turn him from "Doctor Who?" to "Doctor McDreamy" with a style that gets pulses racing in a healthy way.

Materials

Doll and collar
Rowan Cotton Glacé (100% cotton; approx 125yds/115m per 50g ball):
  1 ball in 730 Oyster (A)
  1 ball in 727 Black (B)
  1 ball in 749 Sky (C)
  1 ball in 843 Toffee (D)
Rowan Felted Tweed DK (50% merino wool, 25% alpaca, 25% viscose; approx 191yds/175m per 50g ball):
  1 ball in 181 Mineral (E)
Pair of size 3 (3.25mm) knitting needles
Polyester toy stuffing
Tapestry and embroidery needles
Blue and red embroidery thread for facial features
Sharp sewing needle and thread to match fabric and felt colors if making items below

Lab coat
9 x 12in (23 x 30cm) sheet of white felt fabric

Tie
1³⁄₈ x 6³⁄₄in (3.5 x 17cm) strip of patterned fabric
Press stud

Stethoscope
Small pieces of black and gray felt fabric
5¹⁄₂in (14cm) silver craft wire
Pliers

He'll have you in stitches

Instructions

Doll

Make a basic doll with a tall and slim body shape (page 10) and a side parting hairstyle (page 19), using yarn colors as follows:

Legs: Yarn B, working final row (row 36) of each leg as knit instead of purl to define bottom hem of trousers.

Feet: Yarn D.

Body and head: Use yarn C from pick-up row to end of row 32 of body, then break off C and join in A. Use yarn A to complete neck and head.

Arms and hands: Use yarn C from cast-on to end of row 30 of arms, then break off C and join in A. Use yarn A to work hands.

Soles: Yarn D.

Hair: Yarn E.

Outfit

Using C, make a collar as given for the Sports Star boyfriend on page 108. Pin and stitch collar around neckline of doll, then sew one half of press stud to center front neckline.

Make a long tie (page 44) and sew other half of press stud to WS of knot. Press tie onto doll.

Using white felt, make a lab coat with straight sides and pockets (page 42), then dress the doll.

Stethoscope

Using B, cast on 22 sts.

Bind off 6 sts, slip st used to bind off back onto LH needle, cast on 6 sts, then bind off to end.

Weave in loose ends.

Insert craft wire through top V section of the knitted cord. Making sure that the wire is even, bend the middle to form a V-shape. Use pliers to bend 3/8in (1cm) at ends of wire inward at 90-degree angle.

Cut two 3/8 x 3/4in (1 x 2cm) strips of black felt fabric. Wrap them around bent ends of the wire and stitch to secure.

Cut two 3/8in (1cm) circles from gray felt fabric. Sandwich the loose end of the knitted cord between the circles and sew together.

Yarnagrams

Can you unknot these yarn twisters?

1. LEEDS KENNITT GIN

2. RENT TAPS FRAC

3. BIT TED KNEARD

4. CHATS IN IT EMIT

Answers on page 143

QUIZ

1. **Which romantic couple actually succeeded in tying the knot?**

A. Tristan and Isolde
B. Romeo and Juliet
C. Ben Affleck and J-Lo
D. Lancelot and Guinevere
E. Elizabeth Bennett and Mr Darcy

2. **Which famous knitter starred in the following movies?**

Knitting Hill
Pretty Scarf Woman
Erin Dropastitch
Eat, Purl, Love
Steel Magneedlias

3. **How many calories do you burn by knitting for 30 minutes?**

A. 10
B. 300
C. 55
D. 225
E. A big fat zero

4. **Which of these action heroes would not be seen dead in a balaclava?**

A. Supurlman
B. The Termiknitter
C. The Wool-verine
D. Batman and Bobbin
E. Dewoolition Man

5. **Which of these knitting movies stars Uma Purlman?**

A. *Raiders of the Lost Stitch*
B. *Purlp Fiction*
C. *Lethal Needles Weapon*
D. *The Curse of the Black Purl*
E. *Good Wool Hunting*

Answers on page 143

Skateboarder

Your skater boy will be stoked if you join him carving a half pipe. You'll have to be into graffiti, or the writing could be on the wall.

Materials

Doll
Rowan Cotton Glacé (100% cotton; approx 125yds/115m per 50g ball):
 ball in 725 Ecru (A)
 ball in 727 Black (C)
Rowan Tweed (100% wool; approx 129yds/118m per 50g ball):
 ball in 588 Bainbridge (B)
Rowan Felted Tweed DK (50% merino wool, 25% alpaca, 25% viscose; approx 191yds/175m per 50g ball):
 ball in 160 Gilt (D)
 ball in 181 Mineral (F)
Rowan Fine Tweed (100% wool; approx 98yds/90m per 25g ball):
 ball in 383 Leyburn (E)
Pair of size 3 (3.25mm) knitting needles
Polyester toy stuffing
Tapestry and embroidery needles
Black and red embroidery thread for facial features, plus ecru thread for shoelaces
Crochet hook

Baggy jeans
Old jeans or two 8in (20cm) squares of denim fabric
Sharp sewing needle and black thread

Skateboard
Leftover yarn C from making the doll
Two size 1/2 (2.5mm) double-pointed needles for working i-cord
2 x 6in (5 x 15cm) piece of thick cardboard
2½ x 6¼in (6 x 16cm) piece of blue felt fabric
9 x 12in (23 x 30cm) sheet of black felt fabric
2in (5cm) square of yellow felt fabric
6in (15cm) memory wire or similar
Masking tape and double-sided sticky tape

Instructions

Doll

Make a basic doll with a tall and slim body shape (page 10) and a peaked cut hairstyle (page 20), using yarn colors as follows:

Legs: Yarn B, working final row (row 36) of each leg as knit instead of purl to define bottom hem of trousers.

Feet: Yarn D.

Body and head: Use yarn C from pick-up row to end of row 32 of body, then break off C and join in A. Use yarn A to complete neck and head.

Arms and hands: Use yarn C from cast-on to end of row 10 of arms, then break off C and join in A. Use yarn A to complete arms and hands.

Soles: Yarn D.

Hair: Use yarn E for the hair base and yarn F for the peaked top.

Shoelaces: Use ecru thread to embroider a few straight stitches across top of shoes, then tie the ends into a bow.

Baggy jeans

Using template on page 137, cut two pieces of denim fabric for legs of jeans. Measuring from top edge, mark a point 2¾in (7cm) down both long side edges of each leg. With RS together and using ¼in (5mm) seam allowance and backstitch, sew fabric together from top edge to 2¾in (7cm) marks.

With RS together, align seams at center front and back, then pin and sew down inside leg seams on both legs.

Place jeans inside out on the doll. Fold down the top so that the waistband sits on the doll's waist and pin into position. To hem the legs, fold up the bottom of each leg so that the hems sit just over the shoes and pin into position. Remove jeans from doll and sew waistband and hems in place using backstitch.

Turn RS out and place on doll. To give the jeans a snug fit, pinch the fabric at each side (between waist and hip), and fold toward the back, then pin and sew in place.

This boyfriend also has trousers knitted as part of the basic doll if you don't want to make the jeans, or you could dress him in a pair of slim-fit jeans if you prefer (page 30).

Skateboard

I-cord axle

Using double-pointed needles and C, cast on 4 sts and work i-cord as follows:

Row 1: Knit.

Do not turn; slide the stitches to other end of needle.

Pull yarn tightly across back of work and knit one more row.

Repeat until length is 3¼in (8cm).

Bind off and weave in loose ends.

Board

Using templates on page 138, cut the cardboard section. Insert memory wire lengthways through the middle of the cardboard and trim to fit. This will allow you to fold up one or both ends to shape the skateboard.

Cut the top cover from blue felt fabric. Place a strip of double-sided sticky tape along the cardboard section and stick the blue felt piece centrally on top. Snip the felt around the curved ends (this will allow you to fold and overlap the felt). Fold the felt over the cardboard along each straight edge and secure with masking tape, then do the same around the curved ends. If you don't have masking tape, you can sew the edges of the folded felt together, zigzagging back and forth, to hold them in place.

Cut the bottom cover from black felt (using same template as cardboard). Sew i-cord axle centrally along the black felt.

Wheels

Cut four ⅜ x 6in (1 x 15cm) strips from black felt fabric. Roll up tightly lengthways, then pin and stitch to make inside of wheels.

Cut four ⅜ x 1½in (1 x 4cm) strips from yellow felt fabric. Roll these around the black inner wheels and sew in place.

Place a wheel on each side at the top and bottom of the i-cord axle and sew in place. Pin the black bottom cover and wheels to the underside of the skateboard and stitch in place. Bend up the ends of the board into desired shape.

CELEBRITY KNITTERS

Name these celebrity knitters with their names in neon:

1. Name either of the two stars of the successful vampire movie series who could be found knitting on set.

2. This triple Academy Award winner and grande dame of cinema is no slouch when it comes to singing Abba songs.

3. Which TV actress is "mad" about knitting?

4. Name the *Something About Mary* actress who also loves to knit.

5. One of the stars of *Eat, Pray, Love*, this knitting fan's first movie hit was 1990's *Pretty Woman*. Who is she?

Answers on page 143.

Businessman

Suited and booted, complete with your signature briefcase, this guy is the biz and means it. Make it a meeting of minds and you will be in the money.

Materials

Doll and outfit

Rowan Cotton Glacé (100% cotton; approx 125yds/115m per 50g ball):
1 ball in 843 Toffee (A)
1 ball in 726 Bleached (C)
1 ball in 727 Black (D)
Rowan Pure Wool DK (100% super wash wool; approx 142yds/130m per 50g ball):
1 ball in 003 Anthracite (B)
Pair of size 3 (3.25mm) knitting needles
Polyester toy stuffing
Tapestry and embroidery needles
Black and red embroidery thread for facial features
2 small white shirt buttons, approx ⅜in (1cm) diameter
⅜ x 5¼in (1 x 13cm) strip of pale blue felt fabric for tie
Sharp sewing needle and pale blue thread

Briefcase

Rowan Pure Wool DK (100% super wash wool; approx 142yds/130m per 50g ball):
1 ball in 018 Earth (E)

Two 2.25mm (US 1) double-pointed needles for working i-cord
4in (10cm) square of cardboard

Instructions

Doll

Make a basic doll with a short and slim body shape (page 10) and a short back and sides hairstyle (page 18), using yarn colors as follows:

Legs: Yarn B, working final row (row 30) of each leg as knit instead of purl to define bottom hem of trousers.
Feet: Yarn D.
Body and head: Use yarn C from pick-up row to end of row 32 of body, then break off C and join in A. Use yarn A to complete neck and head.
Arms and hands: Use yarn C from cast-on to end of row 26 of arms, then break off C and join in A. Use yarn A to work hands.
Soles: Yarn D.
Hair: Yarn D.

Shirt collar

Using C, cast on 5 sts.

Knit 2 rows.

Row 3: K1, k2togtbl, k2. (4 sts)

Row 4: Knit.

Row 5: K1, k2togtbl, k1. (3 sts)

Knit 23 rows.

Row 29: K3, m1, k1. (4 sts)

Row 30: Knit.

Row 31: K4, m1, k1. (5 sts)

Knit 2 rows.

Bind off.

Pin center of collar to center back of doll.
Stretch the collar slightly around the
shoulders and neck and pin into position.
Stitch collar in place around neckline.

Suit jacket
Back

Using B, cast on 23 sts.

Knit 2 rows.

Starting with a knit row, work 24 rows in
stockinette stitch.

Place marker at beginning and end of row.

Row 27 (RS): K2, k2togtbl, knit to last
4 sts, k2tog, k2. (21 sts)

Row 28: Purl.

Repeat last 2 rows four times more. (11 sts)

Bind off.

Right front

Using B, cast on 15 sts.

Knit 2 rows.

Row 3 (RS): Knit.

Row 4: P13, k2.

Repeat last 2 rows eight times more.

Row 21: Knit.

Row 22: P12, k3.

Repeat last 2 rows once more.

Row 25: K11, k2tog, k2. (14 sts)

Row 26: P10, k4.

Row 27: K10, k2tog, k2. (13 sts)

Row 28: P9, k4.

Row 29: K9, k2tog, k2. (12 sts)

Row 30: P7, k5.

Row 31: K8, k2tog, k2. (11 sts)

Row 32: P6, k5.

Row 33: K7, k2tog, k2. (10 sts)

Row 34: P5, k5.

Bind off.

Left front

Using B, cast on 15 sts.

Knit 2 rows.

Row 3 (RS): Knit.

Row 4: K2, purl to end.

Repeat last 2 rows eight times more.

Row 21: Knit.

Row 22: K3, purl to end.

Repeat last 2 rows once more.

Row 25: K2, k2togtbl, knit to end. (14 sts)

Row 26: K4, purl to end.

Repeat last 2 rows once more. (13 sts)

Row 29: As row 25. (12 sts)

Row 30: K5, purl to end.

Row 31: As row 25. (11 sts)

Row 32: As row 30.

Repeat last 2 rows once more. (10 sts)

Bind off.

Sleeves (make 2)

Using B, cast on 17 sts.

Knit 2 rows.

Starting with a knit row, work 22 rows in
stockinette stitch.

Place marker at beginning and end of row.
Row 25: K2, k2togtbl, knit to last 4 sts, k2tog, k2. (15 sts)
Row 26: Purl.
Repeat last 2 rows twice more. (9 sts)
Row 31: K2, k2togtbl, k1, k2tog, k2. (7 sts)
Row 32: Purl.
Bind off.

Collar
Using B, cast on 4 sts.
Knit 51 rows.
Bind off.

Finishing
Weave in loose ends. Block and press if required. Using mattress stitch, sew up the armhole seams of body and sleeves between markers. Sew up side seams and sleeves.
Using the photograph as a guide, pin center of collar to center back of neckline. Sew in place, making sure that front edges of collar are positioned symmetrically. Fold back the lapels. Sew buttons to left front edge of jacket below lapel.

Tie
Using illustrations on page 131 as a guide, fold knot at top of pale blue felt fabric to create tie effect. Sew back of tie knot to center front neckline of doll.

Briefcase
Using E, cast on 23 sts.
Starting with a knit row, work 19 rows in stockinette stitch.

Rows 20–22: Knit.
Repeat last 22 rows once more.
Shape top flap as follows:
Row 45: Knit.
Row 46: K2, purl to last 2 sts, k2.
Repeat last 2 rows twice more.
Row 51: K2, k2togtbl, knit to last 4 sts, k2tog, k2. (21 sts)
Row 52: Knit.
Row 53: As row 51. (19 sts)
Bind off 8 sts, k3, bind off to end.
These 3 sts will form front fastening.
Rejoin yarn to 3 sts and knit 5 rows.
Bind off.

Handle
Using double-pointed needles and E, cast on 3 sts and work i-cord as follows:
Row 1: Knit.
Do not turn; slide the stitches to other end of needle.
Pull yarn tightly across back of work and knit one more row.
Repeat until 80 rows have been worked.
Bind off.

Finishing
Weave in loose ends. Block and press if required. Lay out briefcase fabric with WS facing. Cut a piece of thick cardboard to fit inside and fold fabric up like an envelope around it. Using mattress stitch, pin and sew side seams. Sew across top opening, then add a few stitches to front flap. Sew handle to top of briefcase, making sure it is positioned symmetrically.

Fireman

He may be a sweltering hot hero every day for someone else, but when this fireman boyfriend comes home at the end of the day it'll be you who needs a cold shower...

Materials

Rowan Cotton Glacé (100% cotton; approx 125yds/115m per 50g ball):
  1 ball in 843 Toffee (A)
  1 ball in 727 Black (B)
  1 ball in 831 Dawn Grey (D)
Rowan Kid Classic (70% lambswool, 22% kid mohair, 8% polyamide; approx 153yds/140m per 50g ball):
  1 ball in 846 Nightly (C)
Rowan Creative Focus Worsted (75% wool, 25% alpaca; approx 220yds/200m per 100g ball):
  1 ball in 3810 Saffron (E)
Pair of size 3 (3.25mm) and size 2 (3mm) knitting needles
Polyester toy stuffing
Tapestry and embroidery needles
Black and red embroidery thread for facial features, plus brown for stubble
Old pair of beige jeans or 20in (50cm) square of similar fabric
9 x 12in (23 x 30cm) sheets of yellow and gray felt fabric
Sharp sewing needle and thread to match fabric and felt colors
8in (20cm) cord elastic

Instructions

Doll
Using size 3 (3.25mm) needles, make a basic doll with a tall and stocky body shape (page 10), a bald head and stubble (page 27), using yarn colors as follows:
Legs and feet: Yarn A.
Body and head: Use yarn D from pick-up row to end of row 32 of body, then break off D and join in A. Use yarn A to complete neck and head.
Arms and hands: Use yarn D from cast-on to end of row 6 of arms, then break off D and join in A. Use yarn A to complete arms and hands.
Soles: Yarn A.
Stubble: Brown embroidery thread.

Trousers

Using template on page 134, cut front and back of trousers from fabric. If using old pair of jeans, use existing hem and cut to fold line on template.

With RS together and using ¼in (5mm) seam allowance and backstitch, pin and sew side seams and then inside leg seams. If using fabric rather than jeans, fold up ⅝in (1.5cm) at bottom edge of each leg and stitch.

To form channel for elastic at waist, fold down ⅝in (1.5cm) from top edge and press with steam iron. Sew around channel, just above the selvedge, leaving a small gap for elastic to be threaded through.

Visibility strips

Cut two ⅝in (1.5cm) wide strips of yellow felt fabric and two ¼in (5mm) strips of gray felt, each long enough to fit around trouser leg. Pin and stitch a gray strip along center of each yellow strip. Pin and stitch around trouser legs 1in (2.5cm) up from bottom.

Waistband

Attach safety pin to end of elastic. Insert pin into the gap in waistband channel and thread through. Bring ends of elastic together, place trousers on doll, and pull elastic tight so that trousers fit snugly around waist. Knot the ends together and trim off excess elastic.

Jacket

Using templates on pages 134-135, cut out back, two fronts, and two sleeves from fabric. With RS together and using ¼in (5mm) seam allowance and backstitch, pin and sew shoulder seams. Pin sleeves into position, aligning center of sleeves with shoulder seams, and sew in place. Pin and sew side seams, then sleeve seams.

With WS facing, fold up ⅜in (1cm) hem at bottom of jacket and sleeves and stitch to secure. Fold back ⅜in (1cm) at each front edge, then fold again. Press with steam iron and sew using hem stitch. Turn RS out and press again.

Collar

Cut a 1½in (4cm) wide strip of fabric long enough to go around neckline plus ⅜in (1cm) extra for tucking in ends. Fold the fabric lengthways into three sections, like an envelope. Matching center of collar with center of back neck, pin and stitch into position using hem stitch or backstitch. Using point of a knitting needle or similar tool, tuck in open ends of fabric strip to align with front edges of jacket and sew together.

Visibility strips

Sew yellow and gray felt visibility strips around sleeves and bottom of jacket, just above the hems, in the same way as for the trousers.

Boots

Using B, make a pair of boots (page 45).

Helmet

Using size 3 (3.25mm) needles and E, cast on 34 sts.

Work 10 rows in stockinette stitch.

Row 11 (RS): K1, [k2togtbl, k4, k2tog] to last st, k1. (26 sts)

Row 12: Purl.

Row 13: K1, [k2togtbl, k2, k2tog] to last st, k1. (18 sts)

Row 14: Purl.

Row 15: K1, [k2togtbl, k2tog] to last st, k1. (10 sts)

Row 16: Purl.

Break off yarn and thread through sts on needle.

Make brim as follows:

With RS facing and using E, pick up and knit 34 sts along cast-on edge.

Row 1 (WS): Knit.

Row 2: K2, [knit into front and back of next st, k1] to last 2 sts, knit to end. (49 sts)

Row 3: Knit.

Bind off.

Sew up back seam and weave in loose ends.

Hose

Using size 2 (3mm) needles and C, cast on 120 sts.

Bind off.

Nozzle

Using size 3 (3.25mm) needles and B, cast on 6 sts.

Knit 2 rows, then work 6 rows in stockinette stitch.

Row 9: K2, m1, k2, m1, k2. (8 sts)

Knit 2 rows.

Bind off.

Weave in loose ends. Wrap nozzle around one end of hose, with wider bound-off edge of nozzle to the outside. Sew side edges of nozzle together and work a few stitches through nozzle and hose to secure.

Everyone loves a knitted man in uniform

All Time Greatest Knits

Wool You Love Me Tomorrow?
The Shirelles

California Purls
Katy Perry

Weave Only Just Begun
The Carpenters

The Other Row
Jason Merino

*Wool You Still Love Me When
I've Done 64 Rows?*
The Beatles

Counting Rows
OneRepublic

I Like To Knit It
Wool.i.am

To Knit Him Is To Love Him
The Teddy Bears

Oops!.... I Dropped It Again
Britney Spears

Materiwool Girl
Madonna

Hey Boy Hey Purl!
The Chemical Brothers

Another Hole in the Wool
Pink Floyd

Sexuwool Healing
Marvin Gaye

Love Wool Tear Us Apart
Joy Division

It's Knit About The Money
Jessie J

What Makes You Beautiwool
One Direction

Whatever Wool Be, Wool Be
Doris Day

Ply Me a River
Justin Timberlake

Fleece A Jolly Good Fellow
Anonymous

Nerd

Throw away his nerdy old anorak and give this boffin-of-a-boyfriend some classy, geek-chic style. He'll be too busy staring at his computer screen to notice, but do it anyway!

Materials

Doll and sweater

Rowan Cotton Glacé (100% cotton; approx 125yds/115m per 50g ball):
   1 ball in 725 Ecru (A)
   1 ball in 831 Dawn Grey (B)
   1 ball in 727 Black (C)
Rowan Pure Wool DK (100% super wash wool; approx 142yds/130m per 50g ball):
   1 ball in 018 Earth (D)
Rowan Felted Tweed DK (50% merino wool, 25% alpaca, 25% viscose; approx 191yds/175m per 50g ball):
   1 ball in 161 Avocado (E)
Pair of size 3 (3.25mm) knitting needles
Polyester toy stuffing
Tapestry and embroidery needles
Blue and red embroidery thread for facial features

Collar, bow tie, and glasses

6in (15cm) square of checked fabric
2in (5cm) length of 1½in (4cm) wide ribbon
5½in (14cm) cord elastic
Sharp sewing needle and thread to match fabric and ribbon
Reel of Scientific Wire Company silver-plated craft wire, 0.2mm thick

Calculator

Scrap of cardboard for template
4¾in (12cm) square of black felt fabric
2½in (6cm) square of light gray felt fabric
Scraps of green and red felt fabric for buttons
Sharp sewing needle and thread to match felt colors

KNIT 2 TOG
4EVA

Instructions

Doll

Make a basic doll with a short and slim body shape (page 10) and a short back and sides hairstyle (page 18), using yarn colors as follows:

Legs: Yarn B, working final row (row 30) of each leg as knit instead of purl to define bottom hem of trousers.

Feet: Yarn C.

Body and head: Yarn A.

Arms and hands: Yarn A.

Soles: Yarn C.

Hair: Yarn D.

Outfit

Using E throughout, make a raglan sweater (page 34).

To add a collar, cut an $3\frac{1}{4}$ x $4\frac{3}{4}$in (8 x 12cm) rectangle from checked fabric. With RS together, fold in half lengthways. Using $\frac{3}{8}$in (1cm) seam allowance and backstitch, sew short side edges together. Turn RS out, using a knitting needle to push out the points. Press with a steam iron.

Fold collar in half lengthways and press again. Pin raw edge of collar to inside of sweater's neckline, making sure that the points of the collar are evenly spaced at the front. Sew the collar to the sweater.

Dress the doll and give him a tartan bow tie (page 44) and pair of glasses (page 45).

Calculator

Cutting the pieces

Using template on page 132, cut a calculator template from cardboard. Bend top curved section along fold line, then open out flat again. Place cardboard template on black felt fabric and draw around it, adding $\frac{1}{4}$in (5mm) extra all around. Cut around line to make front panel, then repeat for back panel.

Cut a $\frac{3}{8}$ x $1\frac{1}{4}$in (1 x 3cm) rectangle of gray felt for the screen and a $\frac{3}{4}$ x $1\frac{1}{4}$in (2 x 3cm) rectangle of gray felt for the buttons. Cut two $\frac{1}{4}$in (5mm) squares of green felt and two of red felt.

Assembling

Sew screen across top rounded section of front panel, then sew green and red squares to left-hand side and gray button section to right-hand side below the fold line.

Thread tapestry needle with black yarn and work three horizontal and two vertical lines across lower gray panel to create buttons. Using black thread and sewing needle, stitch down the black yarn grid on the button panel. Sandwich cardboard template between front and back panels and pin around outer edge. Sew layers together using backstitch, then bend top screen section at a slight angle.

KNITTING TRIVIA

1. Who were the "tricoteuses"?

   Women paid to attend executions by guillotine in the French Revolution; they would sit and knit throughout.

2. What are you doing if you are tinking?

   Undoing a piece of knitting, one stitch at a time; "knit" backward, duh!

3. What is the current record for speed knitting?

   262 stitches in three minutes, set by a Scottish woman in 2008.

4. What is graffiti knitting, aka yarnbombing?

   Street art that uses knitted or crocheted yarn to decorate street lamps, trees, etc.

5. What is thought to be the earliest knitted garment?

   A sock (it had to be that, or a Christmas jumper with a woolly mammoth on it!), around 300 BCE.

Sports Star

No matter what games he's playing, this sports star boyfriend is constantly on the run. You might as well make him look the part as he does so. On your marks, get set, go!

Materials

Doll and outfit

Rowan Cotton Glacé (100% cotton; approx 125yds/115m per 50g ball):
  1 ball in 730 Oyster (A)
  1 ball in 726 Bleached (B)
Rowan Felted Tweed DK (50% merino wool, 25% alpaca, 25% viscose; approx 191yds/175m per 50g ball):
  1 ball in 154 Ginger (C)
Pair of size 3 (3.25mm) knitting needles
Polyester toy stuffing
Tapestry and embroidery needles
Green and red embroidery thread for facial features
Small white shirt button, approx ³⁄₈in (1cm) diameter

Accessories

Rowan Cotton Glacé (100% cotton; approx 125yds/115m per 50g ball):
  1 ball in 727 Black (D)
  1 ball in 725 Ecru (E)
  1 ball in 831 Dawn Grey (F)
Rowan Handknit Cotton (100% cotton; approx 93yds/85m per 50g ball):
  1 ball in 219 Gooseberry (G)
Two size 1 (2.25mm) double-pointed needles for working i-cord
12in (30cm) craft wire, 1mm thick
Pliers
Reel of Scientific Wire Company silver-plated craft wire, 0.2mm thick
1¹⁄₂in (4cm) square of black felt fabric
Sharp sewing needle and black thread

Game, stitch, and match

Instructions

Doll

Make a basic doll with a tall and slim body shape (page 10) and a curly hairstyle (page 23), using yarn colors as follows:

Legs and feet: Use yarn B from cast-on to end of row 8 as directed. Continue using B to work first 8 rows of stockinette stitch for left leg, but work eighth row in knit instead of purl to define bottom hem of shorts. Break off B and join in A. Starting with a knit row, work 28 rows in stockinette stitch to complete left leg. Break off A and join in B to work left foot. Work right leg and foot in matching colors.

Body and head: Use yarn B from pick-up row to end of row 32 of body, then break off B and join in A. Use yarn A to complete neck and head.

Arms and hands: Use yarn B from cast-on to end of row 6 of arms, then break off B and join in A. Use yarn A to complete arms and hands.

Soles: Yarn B.

Hair: Yarn C.

Outfit

Collar

Using B, cast on 5 sts.
Knit 2 rows.
Row 3: K1, k2togtbl, k2. (4 sts)
Row 4: Knit.
Row 5: K1, k2togtbl, k1. (3 sts)

Knit 25 rows.
Row 31: K1, m1; k2. (4 sts)
Row 32: Knit.
Row 33: K1, m1, k3. (5 sts)
Row 34: Knit.
Bind off.

Placket

Using B, cast on 3 sts.
Knit 9 rows.
Bind off.

Waistband

Using B, cast on 3 sts.
Knit 51 rows.
Bind off.

Finishing

Pin and stitch collar around neckline of doll. Sew shirt button onto placket, then sew placket to center front neckline with button at top. Wrap waistband around body and sew ends together, then sew to body.

Tennis racket

Frame

Using double-pointed needles and B, cast on 3 sts and work i-cord as follows:
Row 1: Knit.
Do not turn; slide the stitches to other end of needle.
Pull yarn tightly across back of work and knit one more row.
Repeat until 80 rows have been worked or length is 10¾in (27cm). Bind off.

Handle grip

Using D, cast on 8 sts.
Work 8 rows in stockinette stitch.

Bind off.

Finishing

Thread the 1mm-thick craft wire through i-cord frame. Using pliers, fold up excess wire and squeeze together, making as flat as possible. Bend into tennis racket shape, with straight handle section approx 1¼in (3cm) long.

Wrap the knitted handle grip around straight handle section of frame and stitch into position.

To add strings, thread tapestry needle with yarn E. Insert needle up through i-cord on one side of frame, just above handle. Take the needle horizontally across to opposite side and insert into i-cord there. Move the needle a little farther along through the i-cord frame and then bring it back out. Repeat this process to add approx 12 horizontal strings up to top of frame. Repeat to add vertical strings, weaving the yarn over and under the horizontal strings.
Fasten off.

Tennis ball

Using G, cast on 3 sts.
Work as follows: K1, [k1, p1] 3 times into next st, [turn and p6, turn and k6] twice, turn and p6, turn and slip 3, k3tog, p3sso st resulting from k3tog, k1, turn, p3tog. Break off yarn, leaving a good length tail, and thread through stitch on needle. Thread tapestry needle with tail from bound-off and sew bobble to form tennis ball. Repeat with cast-on tail.

Trophy

Use yarn F and silver-plated craft wire together throughout trophy pattern.
Cup
Cast on 26 sts.
Starting with a knit row, work 8 rows in stockinette stitch.
Row 9 (RS): K3, k2togtbl, [k2, k2togtbl] to last st, k1. (20 sts)
Row 10: Purl.
Row 11: K2, k2togtbl, [k1, k2togtbl] to last st, k1. (14 sts)
Row 12: Purl.
Row 13: K1, [k2togtbl] to last st, k1. (8 sts)
Starting and ending with a purl row, work 7 rows in stockinette stitch.
Row 21: K2, [m1, k1] to end. (14 sts)
Bind off.
Handle (make 2)
Cast on 10 sts, then bind off.
Finishing
Using mattress stitch and yarn F only, sew side seam of trophy. Mold into shape, then sew handles onto sides.
Cut a 1¼in (3cm) circle of black felt fabric and sew to base of trophy using black thread.

Superhero

He might be amazing at saving the world, but this superhero boyfriend is also the only man who can pull off the impossible: make knitted underpants-over-tights look good!

Materials

Rowan Pure Wool DK (100% super wash wool; approx 142yds/130m per 50g ball):
- 1 ball in 054 Tan (A)
- 1 ball in 018 Earth (B)

Rowan Cotton Glacé (100% cotton; approx 125yds/115m per 50g ball):
- 1 ball in 741 Poppy (C)
- 1 ball in 727 Black (D)
- 1 ball in 849 Winsor (E)

Pair of size 3 (3.25mm) knitting needles
Polyester toy stuffing
Tapestry and embroidery needles
Black and red embroidery thread for facial features
Crochet hook
8in (20cm) craft wire
1¼ x 3¼in (3 x 8cm) piece of turquoise felt fabric
Sharp sewing needle and turquoise thread

Instructions

Doll

Make a basic doll with a tall and stocky body shape (page 10) and a slicked-back hairstyle (page 22), using yarn colors as follows:

Legs and feet: Yarn C.

Body and head: Use yarn C from pick-up row to end of row 32 of body, then break off C and join in A. Use yarn A to complete neck and head.

Arms and hands: Use yarn C from cast-on to end of row 30 of arms, then break off C and join in A. Use yarn A to work hands.

Soles: Yarn D.

Hair: Yarn B.

Saving the world, one dropped stitch at a time

Pants

Using E, cast on 19 sts.
Starting with a knit row, work 6 rows in stockinette stitch.
Row 7 (RS): K1, k2togtbl, knit to last 3 sts, k2tog, k1. (17 sts)
Row 8: P1, p2tog, purl to last 3 sts, p2togtbl, p1. (15 sts)
Repeat last 2 rows twice more. (7 sts)
Row 13: As row 7. (5 sts)
Row 14: P1, p3tog, p1. (3 sts)
Work 2 rows in stockinette stitch.
Row 17: K1, m1, k1, m1, k1. (5 sts)
Row 18: P1, m1, purl to last st, m1, p1. (7 sts)
Row 19: K1, m1, knit to last st, m1, k1. (9 sts)
Repeat last 2 rows twice more. (17 sts)
Row 24: As row 18. (19 sts)
Work 6 rows in stockinette stitch.
Bind off.
Fold up pants with cast-on and bound-off edges together. Sew first 3 rows on each side together to form side seams. Dress the doll in the pants.

Cape

Using E, cast on 13 sts.
Row 1 (RS): Knit.
Row 2: K2, purl to last 2 sts, k2.
Row 3: [K3, m1] twice, k1, [m1, k3] twice. (17 sts)
Row 4: As row 2.
Row 5: Knit.
Row 6: As row 2.
Row 7: K3, m1, k5, m1, k1, m1, k5, m1, k3. (21 sts)
Row 8: As row 2.
Row 9: Knit.
Repeat last 2 rows once more, then row 2 once again.
Row 13: K3, m1, k7, m1, k1, m1, k7, m1, k3. (25 sts)
Knit 2 rows.
Bind off.
Cut two lengths of craft wire ¾in (2cm) longer than side edges of cape. Insert on WS, weaving in and out of garter stitch side edges. Fold over ends of wire and stitch into position to secure. Stitch cape along back neck of doll and bend into desired position.

Mask

Using template on page 132, cut the mask out of felt fabric. Place across doll's face, making sure that eyeholes match up with eyes. Pin and stitch into position at the side edges.

THE IMPURLFECT BOYFRIEND

1. Tells his friends that it isn't serious.

2. His dating profile remains active after exclusive dating status is established.

3. Is not familiar with the concept of putting the seat back down and closing the toilet lid in your apartment.

4. Eats food from your plate without asking first.

5. Owns more moisturizer and fake tan than you do.

6. Is unable to cope when you cry.

7. Insists on updating you on his latest gym session in detail.

8. Is a fussy eater (you will never be able to agree on a wedding menu).

9. Is more interested in social media, theCHIVE, Break or the LADbible than you.

10. Gets fixated on sport to the point of obsession and watches/talks about it endlessly.

11. Doesn't call when he says he will and turns up hours late.

12. Goes into his cave and puts up a No Entry sign.

Hipster

This guy lives and breathes cool. He's an individu-wool. Be prepared for artisanal lattes in shabby chic cafes and leafing through Batman comics.

Materials

Doll
Rowan Cotton Glacé (100% cotton; approx 125yds/115m per 50g ball):
  1 ball in 725 Ecru (A)
  1 ball in 844 Green Slate (B)
  1 ball in 739 Dijon (C)
  1 ball in 741 Poppy (D)
Rowan Felted Tweed DK (50% merino wool, 25% alpaca, 25% viscose; approx 191yds/175m per 50g ball):
  1 ball in 145 Treacle (E)
Pair of size 3 (3.25mm) knitting needles
Polyester toy stuffing
Tapestry and embroidery needles
Black and red embroidery thread for facial features, plus white thread for shoelaces
Crochet hook

Extra-long scarf
Rowan Fine Art (45% wool, 25% polyamide, 20% mohair, 10% silk; approx 437yds/400m per 100g hank):
  1 hank in 306 Lapwing (G)—only a small amount of this yarn is required

Cap
Rowan Cotton Glacé (100% cotton; approx 125yds/115m per 50g ball):
  1 ball in 850 Cobalt (F)

Waistcoat
9 x 12in (23 x 30cm) sheet of gray felt fabric
2 small white shirt buttons, approx 5/16in (7mm) diameter
Sharp sewing needle and gray thread

Instructions

Doll

Make a basic doll with a tall and slim body shape (page 10), a hipster hairstyle (page 24), and a beard (page 27), using yarn colors as follows:

Legs: Yarn B, working final row (row 36) of each leg as knit instead of purl to define bottom hem of trousers.

Feet: Yarn D.

Body and head: Use yarn C from pick-up row to end of row 32 of body, then break off C and join in A. Use yarn A to complete neck and head.

Arms and hands: Use yarn C from cast-on to end of row 10 of arms, then break off C and join in A. Use yarn A to complete arms and hands.

Soles: Yarn D.

Hair and beard: Yarn E.

Shoelaces: Use white thread to embroider a few straight stitches across top of shoes, then tie the ends into a bow.

Extra-long scarf

Using G, cast on 150 sts.
Knit 3 rows.
Bind off and weave in loose ends.

Cap

Using F, make a cap as given for the Hip-Hop Guy boyfriend on page 74, but don't reinforce the underside of the brim with felt fabric.

Waistcoat

Using templates on page 139, cut out back, two fronts and two pocket tops from gray felt fabric.

With RS together and using $1/4$in (5mm) seam allowance and backstitch, pin and sew shoulders and then side seams.

Turn RS out and press with steam iron.

Using picture as a guide, sew a pocket top to each front panel, making sure they are positioned symmetrically. Sew buttons to opening edge of left front panel.

WORKS OF GREAT KNITERATURE

Woolering Heights
Emily Brontë

All's Wool That Ends Wool
William Shakespeare

Stitch-22
Joseph Heller

The Name of the Rows
Umberto Eco

Lady Knitterley's Lover
DH Lawrence

Fifty Shades of Gray Wool
EL James

Harry Knitter and the Goblet of Fire
JK Rowling

Twoolight
Stephenie Meyer

The Arabian Knits
Anonymous

A KNIT AT THE MOVIES

The Talented Mr Knitley
Purl Harbor
Knitted Hat on a Hot Tin Roof
Scarf Face
Apurllo 13
The Dark Knit Rises
Stitch in the City
It's a Wonderpurl Life
The Knitbetweeners
Knitmare on Elm Street

YOUR KNITTED BOYFRIEND'S FAVORITE TV SHOWS

1. Made Men

2. The Knitted Dead

3. The Stitch of It

4. The Big Bind Theory

5. Knit Rider

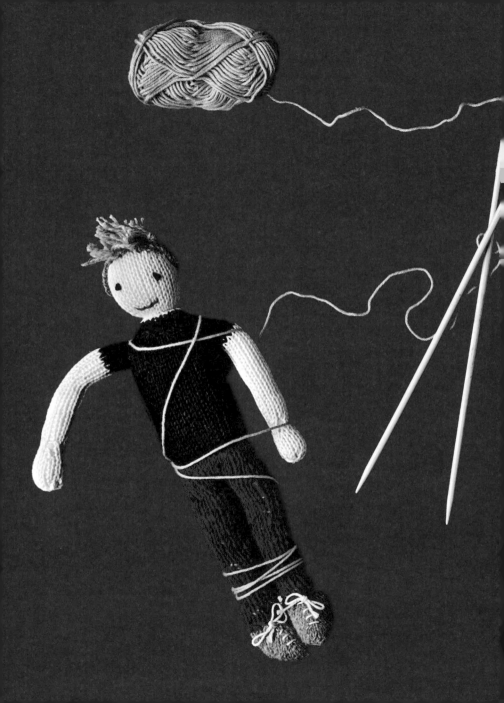

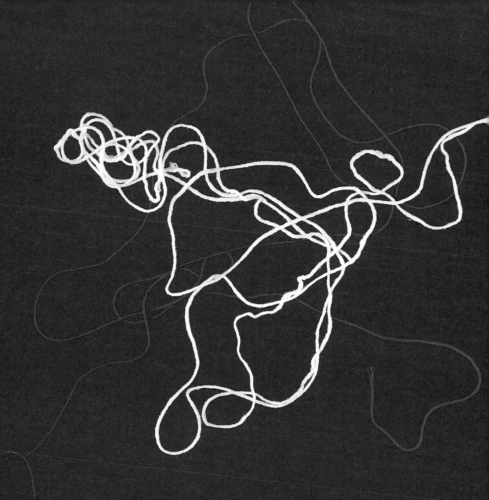

Techniques
and templates

Techniques

Working from a pattern

Before starting any pattern, always read it through. This will give you an idea of how the design is structured and the techniques that are involved. Each pattern includes the following basic elements:

Materials
This section gives a list of materials required, including the amount of yarn, the sizes of needles, and any extras. The yarn amounts specified are based on average requirements and are therefore approximate.

Abbreviations
Knitting instructions are normally given in an abbreviated form, which saves valuable space.
In this book the most commonly used abbreviations are listed on page 144.

Project instructions
Before starting to knit, read the instructions carefully to understand the abbreviations used, how the design is structured, and in which order each piece is worked. However, there may be some parts of the pattern that only become clear when you are knitting them.

Asterisks or square brackets are used to indicate the repetition of a sequence of stitches. For example: *k3, p1; rep from * to end. This means, knit three stitches, then purl one stitch, then repeat this sequence to the end of the row. It could also be written: [k3, p1] to end.

When you put your knitting aside, always mark where you are on the pattern; it is better to be safe than sorry, especially if a complex stitch is involved.

Gauge and selecting correct needle size
Gauge can differ quite dramatically between knitters. This is because of the way that the needles and the yarn are held. If your gauge does not match that stated in the pattern, you should change your needle size following this simple rule:

- If your knitting is too loose, your gauge will read that you have fewer stitches and rows than the given gauge, and you will need to change to a thinner needle, or a smaller needle size, to make the stitch size smaller.
- If your knitting is too tight, your gauge will read that you have more stitches and rows than the given gauge, and you will need to change to a thicker needle, or a larger needle size, to make the stitch size bigger.

Finishing
The finishing section in each project will tell you how to join the knitted pieces together. Always follow the recommended sequence.

Making a slip knot

A slip knot is the basis of all casting-on techniques and is therefore the starting point for almost everything you do in knitting.

1 Wind the yarn around two fingers twice. Insert a knitting needle through the first (front) strand and under the second (back) one.

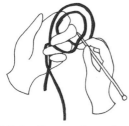

2 Using the needle, pull the back strand through the front one to form a loop. Holding the loose ends of the yarn with your left hand, pull the needle upward, thus tightening the knot.

Casting on: thumb method

Casting on is the term used for making a row of stitches to be used as a foundation for your knitting. The thumb cast-on method produces an elastic edge.

1 Place the slip knot on the needle, leaving a long tail, and hold the needle in your right hand.

2 *Wind the loose end of the yarn around your thumb from front to back. Place the ball end of the yarn over your left forefinger.

3 Insert the point of the needle under the loop on your thumb. With your right index finger, take the ball end of the yarn over the point of the needle.

4 Pull a loop through to form the first stitch. Remove your left thumb from the yarn. Pull the loose end to secure the stitch. Repeat from * until the required number of stitches has been cast on.

Casting on: two-needle method

Also known as cable cast-on, this technique involves using both the knitting needles and gives a firm edge.

1 Make a slip knot about 6in (15cm) from the end of the yarn. Hold the needle with the slip knot in your left hand and the other needle in your right. With the working end of the yarn in your right hand, put the tip of the right-hand needle into the stitch on the left-hand needle.

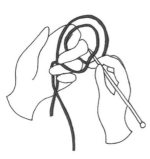

2 Bring the yarn in your right hand under and around the point of the right-hand needle.

3 Pull the yarn taut so that it is wrapped around the tip of the right-hand needle.

4 Bring the tip of the right-hand needle, and the yarn wrapped around it, through the stitch and toward you.

5 Pull gently until the loop is large enough to slip it over the tip of the left-hand needle. Take the right-hand needle out of the loop and pull the working end of the yarn so that the loop fits snugly around the left-hand needle.

6 To cast on all the other stitches, put the tip of the right-hand needle between the last two stitches instead of through the last one. Then repeat steps 2-6 until you have the required number of stitches on the left-hand needle.

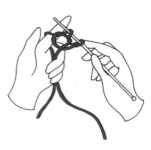

The Basic Stitches

The knit and purl stitches form the basis of all knitted fabrics.

Purl stitch (p)

1 Hold the needle with the stitches in your left hand, with the loose yarn at the front of the work. Insert the right-hand needle from right to left into the front of the first stitch on the left-hand needle. Wrap the yarn from right to left, up and over the point of the right-hand needle.

Knit stitch (k)

1 Hold the needle with the cast-on stitches in your left hand, with the loose yarn at the back of the work. Insert the right-hand needle from left to right through the front of the first stitch on the left-hand needle. Wrap the yarn from left to right over the point of the right-hand needle.

2 Draw the yarn through the stitch, thus forming a new stitch on the right-hand needle. Slip the original stitch off the left-hand needle. To knit a row, repeat until all the stitches have been transferred from the left-hand needle.

2 Draw the yarn through the stitch, thus forming a new stitch on the right-hand needle. Slip the original stitch off the left-hand needle, keeping the new stitch on the right-hand needle. To purl a row, repeat until all the stitches have been transferred from the left-hand needle to the right-hand needle.

Knit through the back of loop (ktbl)

Work as for a knit stitch but insert the right-hand needle from left to right through the back of the first stitch on the left-hand needle.

Purl through the back of loop (ptbl)

Work as a purl stitch but insert the right-hand needle from left to right through the back of the first stitch on the left-hand needle.

Slip stitch

Following the stitch pattern set, insert the right-hand needle into the first stitch on the left-hand needle as if to knit or purl. Transfer it onto the right-hand needle without wrapping the yarn around the right-hand needle to make a new stitch.

Shaping

This is achieved by increasing or decreasing the number of stitches you are working.

Increasing

The simplest method of increasing one stitch is to create two stitches out of one stitch. Work a stitch into the front of the stitch to be increased into; then, before slipping it off the needle, place the right-hand needle behind the left-hand one and work again into the back of it.

Slip the original stitch off the left-hand needle.

Making a stitch (m1)

Another form of increasing involves working into the strand between two stitches.

1 Insert the right-hand needle from front to back under the horizontal strand that runs between the stitches on the right- and left-hand needles.

2 Insert the left-hand needle under the strand from front to back, twisting it as shown, to prevent a hole from forming, and knit (or purl) through the back of the loop. Slip the new stitch off the left-hand needle.

Decreasing (k2tog, k2togtbl, p2tog, p2togtbl)

The simplest method of decreasing one stitch is to work two stitches together.

To knit two stitches together (k2tog), insert the right-hand needle from left to right through the front of the second stitch and then first stitch nearest the tip of the left-hand needle and knit them together as one stitch.

To knit two together through the back of the loops (k2togtbl), insert the right-hand needle from right to left through the back of the first and then second stitch nearest the tip of the left-hand needle and knit them together as one stitch.

To purl two stitches together (p2tog), insert the right-hand needle from right to left through the front of the first and then second stitch nearest the tip of the left-hand needle, then purl them together as one stitch.

To purl two together through the back of the loops (p2togtbl), insert the right-hand needle from left to right through the back of the second and then first stitch nearest the tip of the needle and purl them together as one stitch.

Binding off

This is the most commonly used method of securing stitches once you have finished a piece of knitting. The bound-off edge should have the same "give" or elasticity as the fabric, and you should bind off in the stitch used for the main fabric unless the pattern directs otherwise.

Knitwise

Knit two stitches. *Using the point of the left-hand needle, lift the first stitch on the right-hand needle over the second, then drop it off the needle. Knit the next stitch and repeat from * until all stitches have been worked off the left-hand needle and only one stitch remains on the right-hand needle. Cut the yarn, leaving enough to sew in the end, thread the end through the stitch, then slip it off the needle. Draw the yarn up firmly to fasten off.

Purlwise

Work as for knitwise but purl the stitches rather than knit them.

Sewing Tips

Finishing techniques

You may have finished knitting but there is one crucial step still to come, the sewing up of the seams. It is tempting to start this as soon as you bind off the last stitch but a word of caution: make sure that you have good light and plenty of time to complete the task.

Mattress stitch (side edges)

This stitch makes an almost invisible seam on the knit side of stockinette stitch. Thread a tapestry needle with yarn and position the pieces side by side, right sides facing.

1 Working from the bottom of the seam to the top, come up from back to front at the base of the seam, to the left of the first stitch in from the edge, on the left-hand side and leave a 4in (10cm) tail of yarn. Take the

needle across to the right-hand piece, to the right of the first stitch, and pass the needle under the first two of the horizontal bars that divide the columns of stitches above the cast-on.

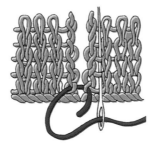

2 Take the needle across to the left-hand piece, insert the needle down where it last emerged on the left-hand edge and pass the needle under two of the horizontal bars that divide the columns of stitches. Take the needle across to the right-hand piece, insert the needle down through the fabric where it last emerged on the right-hand edge and pass the needle under the first two of the

horizontal bars that divide the columns of stitches above the cast-on. Repeat step 2 until the seam has been closed.

Mattress stitch (top and bottom edges)

Thread a tapestry needle with yarn and position the pieces top and bottom, right sides facing outermost. Working right to left, come up from back to front through the center of the first stitch on the right edge of the seam. Take the needle to across the top piece, pass the needle under the two loops of the stitch above, then go down again, through the fabric, where the needle emerged on the lower piece. Repeat with the next stitch to the left.

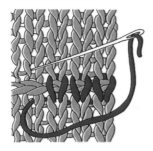

Whip stitch

Thread a tapestry needle with yarn and position the pieces right sides together with the edge to be worked at the top. Working right to left, and always from back to front, pass the needle through the outermost strands of the edge fabric.

Inserting stuffing

As with all soft toys, how you stuff your doll will directly affect the finished appearance.

Stuff firmly, but do not stretch the knitting. Always stuff the extremities, such as the legs and arms, first and mold into shape as you go along. The amount of stuffing needed for each doll depends on the knitting gauge and your individual taste.

Adding detail

Embroidery has been used to add detail to the dolls.

Backstitch

Working from right to left, come up slightly to the left of the start of the line of stitching (A), go down at B and then come up at C. Pull the thread through.

Go down again at B to make a backstitch, then come up at D, ready for the next stitch and then continue to create a solid line of short straight stitches.

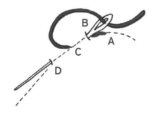

Satin stitch

Work a series of short straight stitches, parallel to each other, to create a pad of stitches.

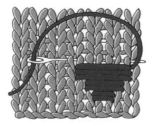

French knots

1 Come up at point A (at which the stitch will sit), wrap the thread twice around the needle in an counterclockwise direction.

2 Push the wraps together and slide to the end of the needle. Go down close to the start point (A), pulling the thread through to form a knot.

Templates

All templates have been reduced to 50% of their size. To enlarge them to the correct size, simply photocopy the pattern using the enlargement button on a photocopier. Photocopy all templates at 200%. You can also find the full-size templates ready to download from www.LoveCrafts.co.uk

Coat (page 42)

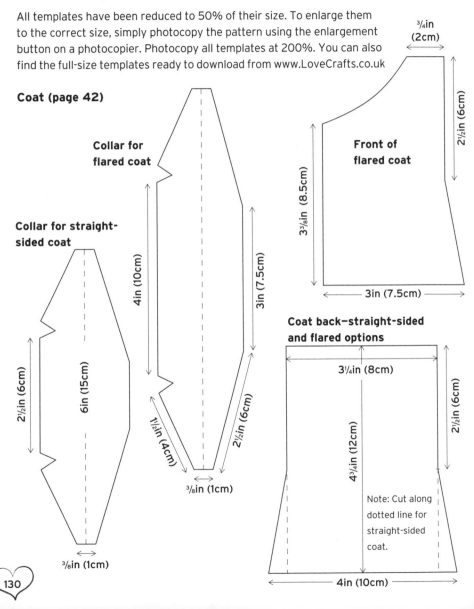

Collar for flared coat

Collar for straight-sided coat

Front of flared coat

¾in (2cm)

2½in (6cm)

3³⁄₈in (8.5cm)

3in (7.5cm)

4in (10cm)

3in (7.5cm)

2½in (6cm)

2½in (6cm)

6in (15cm)

1½in (4cm)

2½in (6cm)

³⁄₈in (1cm)

³⁄₈in (1cm)

Coat back—straight-sided and flared options

3¼in (8cm)

4¾in (12cm)

2½in (6cm)

Note: Cut along dotted line for straight-sided coat.

4in (10cm)

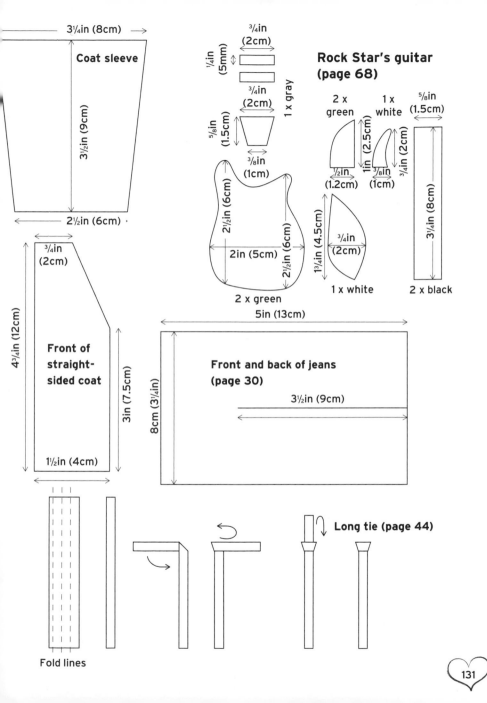

3¼in (8cm) →

Coat sleeve

3½in (9cm)

2½in (6cm)

¾in (2cm)

⅕in (5mm)

¾in (2cm)

⅝in (1.5cm)

⅜in (1cm)

1 x gray

Rock Star's guitar (page 68)

2 x green

1 x white

⅝in (1.5cm)

1in (2.5cm)

¾in (2cm)

½in (1.2cm)

⅜in (1cm)

3¼in (8cm)

2½in (6cm)

2in (5cm)

2½in (6cm)

1¾in (4.5cm)

¾in (2cm)

2 x green

1 x white

2 x black

¾in (2cm)

4¾in (12cm)

Front of straight-sided coat

3in (7.5cm)

1½in (4cm)

5in (13cm)

Front and back of jeans (page 30)

8cm (3¼in)

3½in (9cm)

Long tie (page 44)

Fold lines

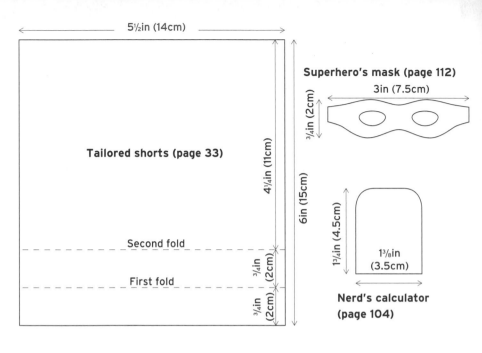

5½in (14cm)

Tailored shorts (page 33)

4¼in (11cm)

6in (15cm)

Second fold

First fold

¾in (2cm)

¾in (2cm)

Superhero's mask (page 112)

3in (7.5cm)

¾in (2cm)

1¾in (4.5cm)

1⅜in (3.5cm)

Nerd's calculator (page 104)

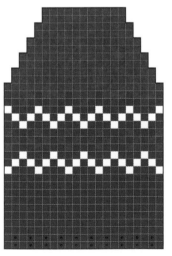

Front and back

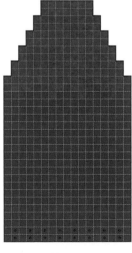

Sleeve

Fair Isle raglan sweater (page 34)

Rowan Pure Wool DK (100% super wash wool; approx 142yds/130m per 50g ball):
   1 ball in 036 Kiss (A)
   1 ball in 013 Enamel (B)
   1 ball in 010 Indigo (C)

Note: Complete neckband using C and instructions on page 35.

■ A
□ B
■ C
■ P on RS, K on WS

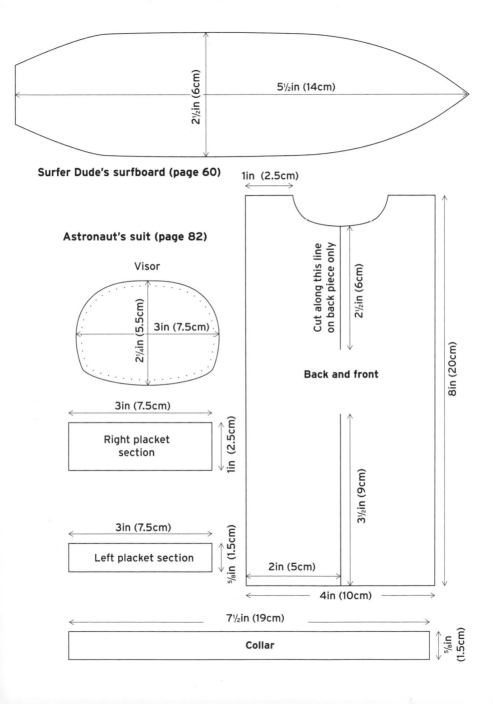

Surfer Dude's surfboard (page 60)

5½in (14cm)

2½in (6cm)

Astronaut's suit (page 82)

Visor

3in (7.5cm)

2¼in (5.5cm)

3in (7.5cm)

Right placket
section

1in (2.5cm)

3in (7.5cm)

Left placket section

⅝in (1.5cm)

1in (2.5cm)

Cut along this line
on back piece only

2½in (6cm)

Back and front

8in (20cm)

3½in (9cm)

2in (5cm)

4in (10cm)

7½in (19cm)

Collar

⅝in (1.5cm)

Fireman (page 98)

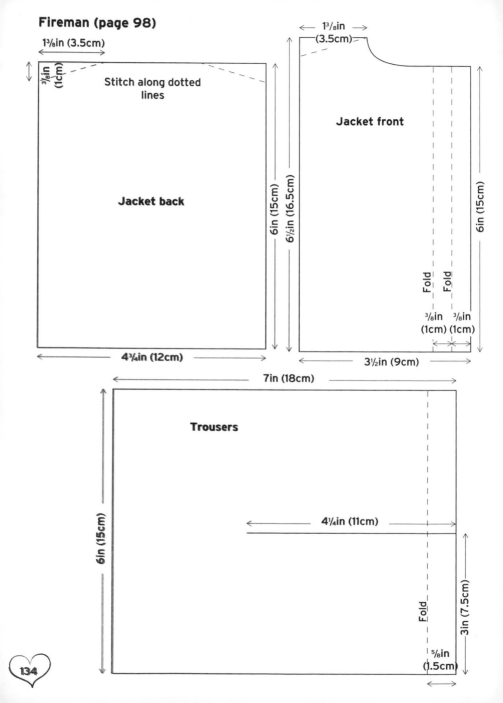

1³⁄₈in (3.5cm)

³⁄₈in (1cm)

Stitch along dotted lines

Jacket back

6in (15cm)

6½in (16.5cm)

4¾in (12cm)

1³⁄₈in (3.5cm)

Jacket front

6in (15cm)

Fold   Fold

³⁄₈in (1cm)   ³⁄₈in (1cm)

3½in (9cm)

7in (18cm)

Trousers

6in (15cm)

4¼in (11cm)

Fold

3in (7.5cm)

⁵⁄₈in (1.5cm)

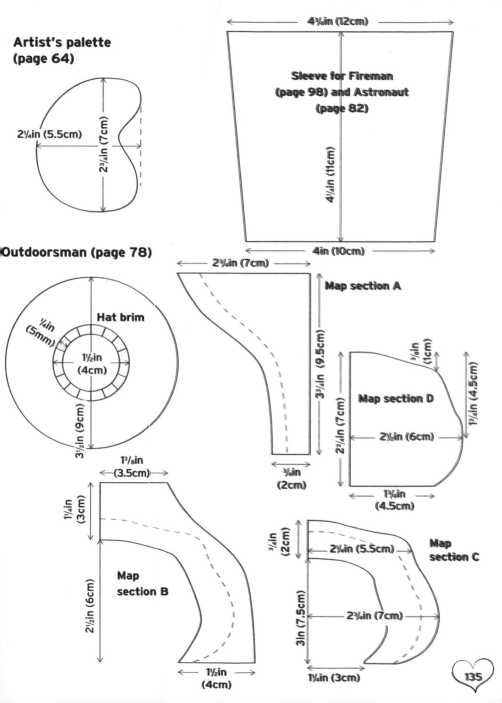

Artist's palette
(page 64)

2¼in (5.5cm)

2¾in (7cm)

4¾in (12cm)

Sleeve for Fireman
(page 98) and Astronaut
(page 82)

4⅓in (11cm)

4in (10cm)

Outdoorsman (page 78)

2¾in (7cm)

Map section A

3¾in (9.5cm)

¾in (2cm)

Hat brim

¼in (5mm)

1½in (4cm)

3½in (9cm)

⅜in (1cm)

Map section D

2¾in (7cm)

1¾in (4.5cm)

2½in (6cm)

1¾in (4.5cm)

1⅜in (3.5cm)

1¼in (3cm)

Map section B

2½in (6cm)

1½in (4cm)

⅜in (2cm)

2¼in (5.5cm)

Map section C

3in (7.5cm)

2¾in (7cm)

1¼in (3cm)

135

Hip-Hop guy (page 72)

T-shirt

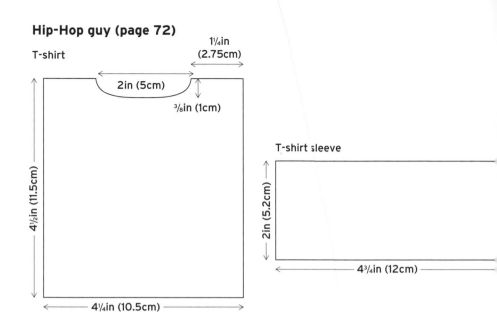

1¼in (2.75cm)

2in (5cm)

³⁄₈in (1cm)

4½in (11.5cm)

4¼in (10.5cm)

T-shirt sleeve

2in (5.2cm)

4¾in (12cm)

Boombox

1¼in (3cm) dark gray

¾in (2cm) light gray

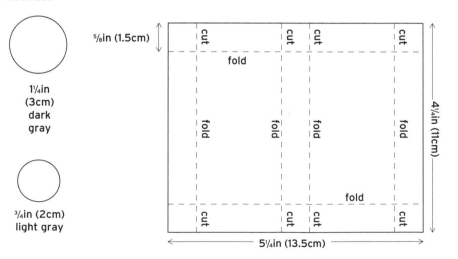

⁵⁄₈in (1.5cm)

cut   cut   cut   cut

fold

fold   fold   fold   fold

fold

cut   cut cut   cut

4¼in (11cm)

5¼in (13.5cm)

Cap lower brim

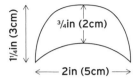

1¼in (3cm)

¾in (2cm)

2in (5cm)

Baggy jeans

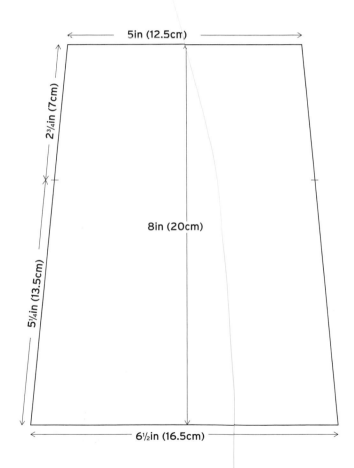

5in (12.5cm)

2¾in (7cm)

8in (20cm)

5¼in (13.5cm)

6½in (16.5cm)

Skateboarder (page 90)

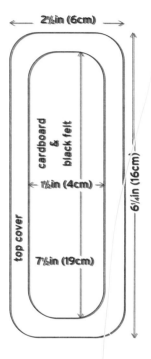

2½in (6cm)

6¼in (16cm)

cardboard & black felt

1½in (4cm)

7½in (19cm)

top cover

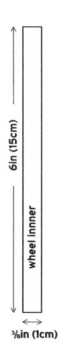

6in (15cm)

wheel innner

⅜in (1cm)

wheel outer

4cm

⅜in (1cm)

Hipster (page 116)

waistcoat

pocket

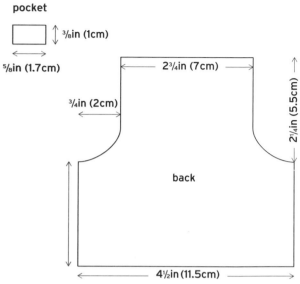

¾in (2cm)

¾in (2cm)

2½in (6cm)

2½in (5.5cm)

2in (5cm)

2½in (6cm)

front

⅜in (1cm)

⅝in (1.7cm)

2¾in (7cm)

¾in (2cm)

2¼in (5.5cm)

back

4½in (11.5cm)

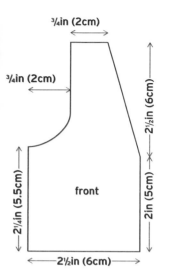

Sports Fan (page 56)

¾in (2cm)

1¾in (4.5cm)

1¾in (4.5cm)

¾in (2cm)

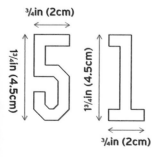

Smart jacket
(page 39)

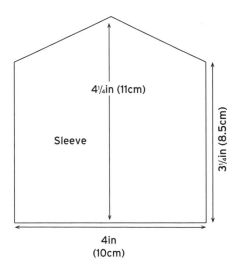

Sleeve

4¼in (11cm)

3¼in (8.5cm)

4in
(10cm)

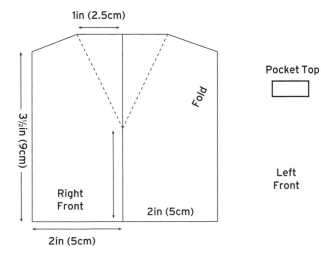

1in (2.5cm)

3½in (9cm)

Fold

Right
Front

2in (5cm)

2in (5cm)

Pocket Top

Left
Front

2in (5cm)

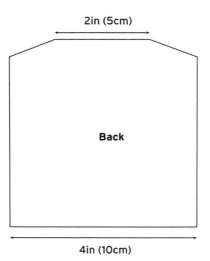

Back

4in (10cm)

Don't String your Boyfriend Along

You've knitted him, but it's important not to lose him.

1. Don't cast him out or off without talking it through.
2. Don't let your relationship unravel through being casual.
3. Don't spin a yarn about washing your hair when you're knot.
4. Spend time unwinding together.
5. Remember, it takes balls to be a good knitter.

Answers

Celebrity knitters (page 93)
1. Dakota Fanning and Kristen Stewart, stars of *Twilight*
2. Meryl Streep
3. Christina Hendricks, star of *Mad Men*
4. Cameron Diaz
5. Julia Roberts

Quiz (page 89)
1. Elizabeth Bennett and Mr Darcy (E)
2. Julia Roberts
3. 55 (C)
4. The Termiknitter (B)
5. Purlp Fiction (B)

Yarnagrams (page 88)
1. Knitting needles
2. Scarf pattern
3. Knitted beard
4. A stitch in time

Abbreviations

approx	approximately
cm	centimeter(s)
g	gram(s)
in	inch(es)
k	knit
k2tog	knit two stitches (or number stated) together
k2togtbl	knit two stitches (or number stated) together through back of loops
LH	left hand
m	meter(s)
m1	make one stitch
mm	millimeter(s)
oz	ounce(s)
p	purl
p2sso	pass two (or number stated) slipped stitches over
p2tog	purl two stitches (or number stated) together
p2togtbl	purl two stitches (or number stated) together through back of loops
psso	pass slipped stitch over
RH	right hand
RS	right side
st(s)	stitch(es)
tbl	through back of loop
tog	together
WS	wrong side
yd(s)	yard(s)
[ ]	work directions within square brackets as directed